||||| ||| ||||||| ||||| ||| |||| ||| |||||

W9-BAH-234

Chuck Tomasi
Kreg Steppe

*Wordpress forums*

## Sams **Teach Yourself**

# WordPress

## in **10 Minutes**

**SAMS** | 800 East 96th Street, Indianapolis, Indiana 46240

Sams Teach Yourself WordPress in 10 Minutes

Copyright © 2010 by Pearson Education, Inc.

ISBN-13: 978-0-672-33120-6

ISBN-10: 0-672-33120-9

Library of Congress Cataloging-in-Publication Data

Tomasi, Chuck.

  Sams teach yourself WordPress in 10 minutes / Chuck Tomasi and Kreg Steppe.

     p. cm.

  Includes index.

  ISBN 978-0-672-33120-6

  1.  WordPress (Electronic resource) 2.  Blogs—Computer programs. 3.  Web sites—Design—Computer programs. I. Steppe, Kreg. II. Title.

  TK5105.8885.W66T65 2010

  006.7'8—dc22

                     2010005881

Printed in the United States of America

Second Printing  April 2010

**Trademarks**

All terms mentioned in this book that are known to be trademarks or service marks have been appropriately capitalized. Pearson Education, Inc. cannot attest to the accuracy of this information. Use of a term in this book should not be regarded as affecting the validity of any trademark or service mark.

**Warning and Disclaimer**

Every effort has been made to make this book as complete and as accurate as possible, but no warranty or fitness is implied. The information provided is on an "as is" basis. The author and the publisher shall have neither liability nor responsibility to any person or entity with respect to any loss or damages arising from the information contained in this book.

**Bulk Sales**

Pearson offers excellent discounts on this book when ordered in quantity for bulk purchases or special sales. For more information, please contact

  **U.S. Corporate and Government Sales**
  **1-800-382-3419**
  corpsales@pearsontechgroup.com

For sales outside of the U.S., please contact

  **International Sales**
  international@pearsoned.com

**Associate Publisher**
Greg Wiegand

**Acquisitions Editors**
Laura Norman
Rick Kughen

**Development Editor**
Wordsmithery, LLC

**Managing Editor**
Patrick Kanouse

**Project Editor**
Seth Kerney

**Copy Editor**
Chuck Hutchinson

**Proofreader**
Water Crest Publishing

**Indexer**
Ken Johnson

**Technical Editor**
Yvonne Johnson

**Publishing Coordinator**
Cindy Teeters

**Book Designer**
Anne Jones

**Compositor**
Mark Shirar

# Contents at a Glance

# Contents

# About the Authors

**Chuck Tomasi** is an IT manager for Plexus Corp., a contract electronics company head-quartered in Neenah, Wisconsin. He has almost 30 years of IT experience and is also a devoted husband and proud father of two. Chuck is an accomplished writer and public speaker on New Media. His first book, *Podcasting for Dummies* (co-written with Tee Morris and Evo Terra), was ranked #1 by Neilsen BookScan in its category. He is a regular contributing writer to the Friends In Tech and Tech Talk for Families blogs. Chuck is a pioneer in podcasting who began working with the media in 2004 when it was still in its infancy. He is the co-host of the light-hearted weekly tech/science podcast Technorama, which was a finalist in two categories at the 2007 Parsec Awards for podcasting excellence. He also produces and hosts the Gmail Podcast, a collection of short audio tips. As a speaker, Chuck has led training sessions on podcasting for the National Park Service, spoken at the New Media Expo on how to build listener loyalty, presented a session at the National HDI (Help Desk Instutite) conference on effective customer communications, and done numerous presentations for his local HDI chapter. Chuck is also the founder, host, and regular presenter for Fox Cities Managers, a local group of professionals dedicated to leadership excellence in northeast Wisconsin.

Find out more about Chuck at http://www.chucktomasi.com.

**Kreg Steppe** has 20 years of experience as an IT professional. Kreg is a husband and father of one. He has several interests in creative writing, photography, audio production, and web application development. Currently working as a web developer, he has 10 years experience with web technologies including HTML, JavaScript, PHP, MySQL, Apache, and IIS. His work leads him to create rich and robust solutions including writing a custom intranet, extranet, and workflow applications. He is also a podcasting early adopter. In late 2004, as podcasting started to get recognition, Kreg became involved with several podcasts, emerging as a consummate assistant to budding podcasters. In early 2005 Kreg joined Chuck Tomasi and launched Technorama, a podcast with a lighthearted look at all things tech and sci-fi. Working on Technorama, and as a member of Friends In Tech podcasting group, Kreg has had several years of audio production experience including creative writing, coordination logistics, and editing. Most recently, Kreg spoke at Create South 2009 regarding "Sharing Your Photography and Social Media" as an amateur photographer and with an interest in social networking (http://www.kregsteppe.com).

# Dedications

I dedicate this book to my wife, Donna, who has provided the encouragement, time, and support to allow me to realize my goals. To my daughters Julie and Liisa—the light of my life. To my parents, who provided a solid foundation of values and inspire me to keep reaching higher. I love you all very much. —Chuck Tomasi

I dedicate this book to my family, who are all a source of encouragement and motivation. To my wife Kim, who has constantly pushed my boundaries and shown me I can do things that I didn't think possible before. To my son Harrison, who is an endless inspiration. To my parents, who also have shown that hard work and character pay off in the long run. I thank and love you all. —Kreg Steppe

# Acknowledgments

From Chuck, special thanks to Tee Morris for ushering me in to the world of writing. Thanks to Kreg Steppe, who convinced me to stop spending my time writing my own blog software and start using WordPress.

From both of us, our eternal gratitude to Laura, Charlotte, Rick, and everyone behind the scenes at Pearson who helped shape raw knowledge into useful, educational information.

# We Want to Hear from You!

As the reader of this book, *you* are our most important critic and commentator. We value your opinion and want to know what we're doing right, what we could do better, what areas you'd like to see us publish in, and any other words of wisdom you're willing to pass our way.

You can email or write me directly to let me know what you did or didn't like about this book—as well as what we can do to make our books stronger.

*Please note that I cannot help you with technical problems related to the topic of this book, and that due to the high volume of mail I receive, I might not be able to reply to every message.*

When you write, please be sure to include this book's title and author as well as your name and phone or email address. I will carefully review your comments and share them with the author and editors who worked on the book.

Email:     consumer@samspublishing.com

Mail:      Greg Wiegand
           Associate Publisher
           Sams Publishing
           800 East 96th Street
           Indianapolis, IN 46240 USA

# Reader Services

Visit our website and register this book at informit.com/register for convenient access to any updates, downloads, or errata that might be available for this book.

# Introduction

Blogging has been booming for years, and it shows no sign of slowing down. It is an easy and organized way to deliver news, tutorials, and podcasts; it's even an easy way to share personal thoughts and stories. It was the social network before other social networks existed. Like blogging, WordPress has grown over the years to a mature platform that is accessible to everyone, including you. Starting your own blog can be a fun and rewarding experience, but getting there might take a little work. Navigating your way through installation, profile accounts, themes, and plug-ins will be easier after you complete the lessons in this book. You will have all the knowledge you need to start your own blog right away.

## About This Book

As part of the *Sams Teach Yourself in 10 Minutes* guides, this book shows you all the caveats of setting up a blog with WordPress either as a hosted blog or on your personal website. All the topics are separated into easy-to-handle lessons that you can complete in 10 minutes or less. The lessons cover the following tasks and topics:

- ▶ Creating a blog at WordPress.com or installing your blog on another server
- ▶ Configuring and customizing your blog
- ▶ Writing blog posts and pages
- ▶ Mapping your way around the WordPress Dashboard
- ▶ Adding media to your posts
- ▶ Installing themes and plug-ins
- ▶ Customizing widgets
- ▶ Drawing attention to your blog
- ▶ Making your WordPress blog search engine-friendly
- ▶ Blogging on the go

# Who This Book Is For

*Sams Teach Yourself WordPress in 10 Minutes* is for individuals who want to create and operate a personal weblog or website for an organization using WordPress. WordPress is one of the most popular blogging systems, but uninitiated users might need help getting started with it. There are a lot of options and choices to be made within the software. Do you want to host a personal blog or a blog for a business? Maybe you want to show off your photography, or maybe you want to use WordPress to start a podcasting site. WordPress can do all these things, and it includes something for everyone. The advice in this book can make your foray into blogging with WordPress more satisfying.

Each lesson focuses on a particular subject such as installation or managing comments. You can skip around from lesson to lesson or follow through the entire book from beginning to end.

# What You Need to Use This Book

To use this book, you first need a can-do attitude and the curiosity to learn something new. You probably already have the tools you need to start using WordPress: an Internet connection, a computer, and a web browser. If you have those, you are ready to go.

You might also need a credit card or some other payment type to purchase your own domain, and you might need to subscribe to hosting services if you want to host your own WordPress site. You can learn more about these things in Lesson 8, "Setting Up Hosting."

# Conventions Used in This Book

Whenever you need to watch for something in particular or are directed to click on something, those items will appear as **bolded** text, such as "Click on the orange **Download** button." There are also some special sidebars that call out Tips, Notes, and Cautions.

TIP: Tips are nuggets of information that are good to know as you proceed. Tips might also offer shortcuts for getting things done.

NOTE: Notes are extra information that might give you a deeper understanding of a topic and help you expand your knowledge.

CAUTION: Cautions are warnings that alert you to possible consequences or an outcome of using a particular task or feature.

# Screen Captures

The screen captures in this book were taken using the Firefox web browser. If you use a different web browser, your screens might look slightly different.

Also keep in mind that the WordPress developers are constantly at work, and new releases and updates are frequently available. Often new features are added or pages are slightly redesigned. These updates mean that the screen captures in this book might differ a little from what you see when using WordPress. Just remember: Don't panic. Even though things change regularly over time, the basic principles and functionality are the same.

# LESSON 1

# Introducing WordPress

*In this lesson, you learn the basics of WordPress, different ways you can run WordPress, and ways to create your account on WordPress.com.*

## Understanding What WordPress Is

WordPress is a powerful blog (short for web log) publishing system and content management system that is simple to set up and use. You can set up and manage your entire blog from any web browser. You don't need to be a web programmer or have a degree in information technology to start using it. All you need to know is how to log in, type your content, and click a button so the world can read your masterpiece.

So why should you use WordPress for your blog or—as many people have done—as the framework for your entire website? The answer is simple: It is easy to use, expandable, and affordable, and it offers a great community of support. Consider the following personal example.

Recently, our local chapter of a national organization recognized it was time to update its website. The content was fairly static. We would update it once or twice a month to announce the next meeting. Furthermore, our webmaster was the only one who could make changes to the content, and he was available for limited hours each week. Taking a cue from another chapter in our region, we looked at WordPress. It allows for more dynamic content, allowing any of the chapter board members to contribute and manage the content. Dynamic content leads to frequent readers, and having frequent readers (it is hoped) leads to more chapter members. WordPress worked for our neighbor, and it worked for us. Within a couple of months of our conversion to WordPress, our website was a thriving community with comments and conversations. As we had hoped, memberships also rose. The website was no longer an afterthought; it was at the core of how we communicated with our members.

# Options for Using WordPress

WordPress comes in three basic modes: WordPress.com, WordPress.org, and WordPress MU (multiuser). Each one is described in this section so that you can decide which is right for you.

WordPress.com is what's known as a "hosted" solution, meaning a lot of the heavy lifting of installing and configuring the software has been taken care of for you. The benefits of this solution are that it is free and it doesn't take long to start using. You don't need to worry about paying for hosting, running a web server, or downloading software updates. You just create an account, name your blog, and start creating content. The drawback is that WordPress.com is not always as flexible as some people like. For example, you cannot install themes and plug-ins, run ads, or edit the database. To start using WordPress.com, visit its site at http://wordpress.com.

> NOTE: Although WordPress.com is a free service, it is financially supported by optional paid upgrades, VIP services, and Google AdSense advertising.

The second way to use WordPress is to download and install the software yourself from WordPress.org. This task requires a little more technical savvy (and money). The advantage is that you have more control over the appearance and functionality of the way your site is run. The additional flexibility, though, creates additional complexity. Don't worry; installing your own WordPress is not all that daunting, and you can read more about it in Lesson 10, "Installing WordPress." With this option, you need to pay for web hosting, so you can shop around for the service that best fits your needs. You need to ensure your hosting provider has PHP version 4.3 or greater (the programming language WordPress is built on) and MySQL version 4.1.2 or greater (the database behind WordPress).

The final way to run WordPress is to use WordPress MU (multiuser). It is the same software that runs WordPress.com, but it's meant for large organizations such as schools, networks, or companies that want to run dozens of blogs under one central administration. The use of WordPress MU is beyond the scope of this book. If you want more information on WordPress MU, you can find it at http://mu.wordpress.org.

# WordPress Features

There are several reasons to consider WordPress instead of other blogging software sites or packages.

WordPress is extensible, meaning you can start with a basic setup and add on many plug-ins to extend the functionality of your software (see Table 1.1). The capabilities of plug-ins range from taking a simple poll to distributing audio and video files with your regular content. The official repository of WordPress plug-ins is available at http://wordpress.org/extend/plugins/.

One nice feature about WordPress is that you can always start simple with WordPress.com. Then, if you decide you want to extend your features beyond what WordPress.com can offer, you can migrate it later to your own website using the software downloaded from WordPress.org. If you think you might one day migrate from WordPress.com to your own web-site, there are some factors you should take in to account. We talk about them in Lesson 8, "Using RSS and Data Migration Tools."

Table 1.1    WordPress.org and WordPress.com Feature Comparison

| Feature | WordPress.org | WordPress.com |
| --- | --- | --- |
| Cost | Free | Free |
| Requires hosting | Yes | No |
| Requires download | Yes | No |
| Requires setup/installation | Yes | No |
| Ability to install your own templates | Yes | No |
| Ability to use sidebar widgets | Yes | Yes |
| RSS | Yes | Yes |
| Ability to install plug-ins | Yes | No |
| Ability to set up multiple blogs with one account | No | Yes |
| Customizable style sheets | Yes | $15/year |

PLAIN ENGLISH:   **RSS**

RSS stands for Really Simple Syndication. It is a method that computers use to exchange information. For the purposes of WordPress, RSS allows people to "subscribe" to your blog, much like they subscribe to a magazine. Rather than people coming to your site to check for new content, an application periodically checks all subscribed sites (also known as "feeds") for new content and presents it much like email. RSS functionality is being incorporated in many popular applications such as Microsoft Outlook and Internet Explorer. It is available in specialized applications, called RSS readers, such as Mozilla Thunderbird. There are even RSS readers available as web applications—such as Google Reader—and several for your iPhone.

WordPress has a large community of fiercely loyal followers that provide an excellent support network. If you have questions, you are likely to find the answers at http://wordpress.org/support or http://codex.wordpress.org. If you cannot find answers to your questions in this book, the Codex website is an excellent resource.

### The History of WordPress

Although WordPress was one of three leaders in both rate of adoption and brand strength as measured in the 2009 Open Source Content Management System Market Share Report, it had its humble beginnings just a few short years ago. In early 2003, a young man by the name of Matt Mullenweg found that his favorite publishing software (called b2) was without a lead developer. He decided to take up the task to enhance and rebrand b2 as WordPress. He was soon joined by Mike Little and the original b2 developer, Michael Valdrighi. A few months later, the first release of WordPress was made available. In August 2006, the software had more than 1 million downloads. In 2007, that number reached 3 million.

**Have a Strategy**

Before you start using WordPress, it pays to have a vision, or a plan, of what you want your blog to be. Is this something for friends and family to keep up with, or is it a publication for an organization you belong to? Do you have a theme or brand to adhere to, or are you allowed to experiment? Do you have a name for your blog? All these issues should be considered before you dive in.

# Getting Started with WordPress.com

Here's an example of how easy it is to start using WordPress. Let's assume you have been tasked with creating a website for your local chapter martial arts club.

To start with WordPress.com, follow these steps:

1.  Go to the main WordPress.com site at http://wordpress.com.

2.  Click the **Sign Up Now** button.

3.  Create a user name and password, and fill in the email address. Be sure to review the terms of service and check the box that states you have read and agree to them. Click **Next**. See Figure 1.1.

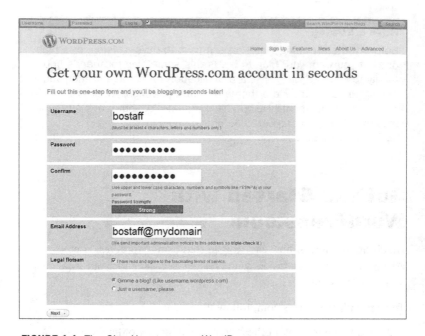

**FIGURE 1.1** The Sign Up screen on WordPress.com.

4. Name your blog. The blog domain is the web address where people will find your blog. By default, it is the same name as your user name. Change the blog domain if you want to use a web address different than your user name. The Blog Title is the name of your blog. You can change this at any time in the blog settings. Select the language your blog uses and choose your privacy option. Finally, click **Sign Up**. See Figure 1.2. For our example, I used the blog domain bostaff.wordpress.com, the title "Fox Cities Martial Arts," left the language as English, and chose to make the blog visible to search engines.

---

CAUTION: **Choosing Your Blog Domain**

Choose your blog domain carefully. Once it is set, it cannot be changed.

---

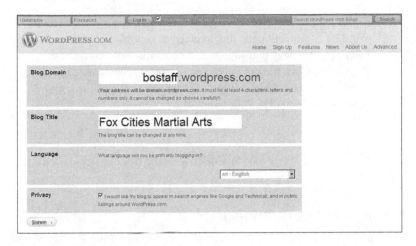

**FIGURE 1.2** Choose your blog address and title.

5. Update your profile. Enter your first name, last name, and little text about yourself. When you are done, click **Save Profile**. See Figure 1.3.

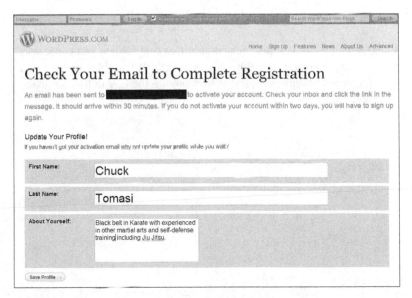

**FIGURE 1.3** Include a little more information in your profile.

6. Check your email. When you get the confirmation message from
   WordPress.com, click the link to activate your blog. The link
   takes you to a page that says Your Account Is Now Active. See
   Figure 1.4. Click the link on the page to view your site or log in.
   Until you receive the email and click on the link, you cannot
   publish any content to your blog.

**FIGURE 1.4** After your account is active, you can log in and start creating
content.

7. Click View Your Site.

Congratulations, you've just created your first blog! When you come back
to WordPress.com, you can either log in directly at your blog address—for
example, http://bostaff.wordpress.com—and use the Log in link, or go to
http://wordpress.com.

# Migrating From Another Blog

If you already have a blog with another popular site or software, WordPress makes it possible to migrate your content. Currently, you can import from any of the following blogs:

- ► Blogger
- ► LiveJournal
- ► Movable Type or TypePad
- ► WordPress
- ► Yahoo! 360

See Lesson 8 for more information on migrating your blog to WordPress.com.

# Summary

In this lesson, you learned what WordPress is and how it can be used. You also learned how quickly and easily you can log in to WordPress.com and create your own account.

# LESSON 2

# Completing Your Profile

*In this lesson, you learn the value of setting up your profile, where to locate your personal profile, how to set the various options, and what each option does.*

## Finding Your Profile

NOTE: **Profile Differences Between WordPress.com and WordPress.org**

The profile options mentioned in this lesson apply to WordPress.com. Where necessary, exceptions for WordPress.org users are noted.

Let's begin by finding your profile. If you are not already logged in to WordPress.com, start by taking one of the following steps:

▶ Go to http://wordpress.com, log in, and click the **Dashboard** link under the name of your blog.

▶ Go to http://yoursite.wordpress.com, click the **Log in** link, and enter your login ID and password. If your browser remembers you from a previous session, click the **Site Admin** link.

After you are logged in, look at the side menu on the left and scroll down if necessary to locate the section labeled Users. As you move your cursor over the Users label, a downward-pointing triangle will appear. Click the triangle to expand the menu options. In that list, click **Your Profile**. Your screen should now look similar to the one shown in Figure 2.1.

The API key is blocked

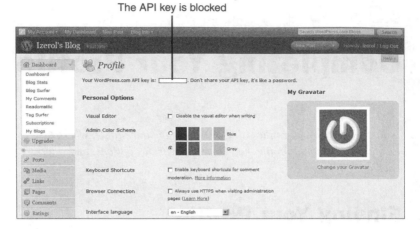

**FIGURE 2.1**   Taking the time to set the various options in your profile gives your blog a more polished look.

# Profile Options

Your user profile contains several options to help manage and personalize your blog including personal preferences, contact information, and how you would like to be represented online. The information in your user profile applies to all the blogs you own on WordPress.com. Most of the information in your user profile is not displayed publicly.

## Your Personal API Key

The first item displayed at the top of the profile screen is your Personal API key. This key is your personal identifier to the WordPress.com system. It allows the system to identify you if you choose to use services and enhancements the system has to offer, even if you host your blog elsewhere. It is generated automatically when you create your WordPress.com account. Treat the API key like a password and do not share it. The most popular use of the API key is with the WordPress antispam service Akismet. You can find more details about Akismet in Lesson 5, "Managing Comments."

PLAIN ENGLISH:  **API**

API stands for Application Programming Interface. It is a method by
which programmers allow other programmers to access to his software so that a program that they write can enhance or extend the
functionality of the original program.

# Personal Options

The Personal Options section of the user profile defines the basics of how
you interact with WordPress. Options include the color scheme for the
administrative interface, the image you present to the world, and even
what language you use.

## Visual Editor

The Visual Editor setting allows you to turn on or off the enhanced functionality of the editor when you are composing content such as a blog
posting or page. I recommend leaving this box unchecked so that you can
see the text you create much as it will be displayed when the reader reads
it. The Visual Editor operates much like most common word processors
do with WYSIWYG ("wizzy-wig," which stands for What You See Is
What You Get) functionality. For example, when you click the icon for a
bulleted list, you see a list of bullets in the editor window. If you uncheck
Visual Editor, the icons change to Hypertext Markup Language (HTML)
tags, and you aren't able to edit your text unless you understand HTML,
which is beyond the scope of this book. If you do know HTML, you can
still see it and manipulate it even with the Visual Editor enabled.

## Admin Color Scheme

The Admin Color Scheme option gives you a choice of using blue or gray
highlights and borders in your WordPress admin screens. This is a personal preference. Choose whichever you feel most comfortable with.

## Keyboard Shortcuts

Keyboard Shortcuts were introduced in 2008 to help you rapidly manage
comments using your keyboard instead of several mouse clicks. By
default, Keyboard Shortcuts is turned off, so if your blog gets a lot of
comments or you manage them en masse, you might want to consider

turning it on. To turn on Keyboard Shortcuts, check the box next to **Enable Keyboard Shortcuts for Comment Moderation**. Read more about comments and moderating them in Lesson 5.

---

**Missing Options?**

This book is based on WordPress version 2.9. WordPress.com users are automatically upgraded to the latest version of software. WordPress.org users need to upgrade themselves. If you do not see some of the options mentioned in this book, you should upgrade your WordPress software to the latest version.

---

## Browser Connection

To enable an encrypted connection between your browser and the server when you manage your blog or its settings, which is recommended, check the **Always Use HTTPS When Visiting Administration Pages** box. By default, this option is disabled (unchecked). Although enabling this option is not mandatory, it is a good idea, particularly when you reset user passwords. Without the feature enabled, all information is passed between your computer and the WordPress.com server in "clear format," meaning anyone with moderate technical skills could listen to your conversation. If you enable this feature, all traffic between your browser and the server is encrypted, so anyone listening gets a garbled message.

## Interface Language

WordPress.com supports a wide variety of languages. When you select a language, all the settings, application labels, and other features of WordPress.com are translated. Changing the Interface Language setting does not modify the language in which the content is presented, so if your posts are written in English, changing the interface language to French will not translate your postings.

## Primary Blog

As mentioned in Lesson 1, "Introducing WordPress," WordPress.com allows you to operate multiple blogs from the same account. The Primary Blog setting in your profile lets you specify one blog as your primary blog, which is the default blog displayed when you look at stats and other information in the Global Dashboard.

## Proofreading

The Proofreading section allows you to enable and disable certain types of grammatical checks the Visual Editor performs when you click the **ABC Check** button. Depending on what options you choose in your profile, the proofreading feature will catch or ignore these. For example, checking the Clichés option instructs the proofreader to underline phrases such as "Have a nice day."

The same button can also check for spelling errors and make style suggestions. For example, say you enable the proofreading feature and later type the sentence **I got all the way threw the test without a mistake.** Clicking the ABC Check button runs the proofreader and identifies the word *threw* as a possible mistake and allows you to correct it. When you click the underlined word, the proofreader makes the suggestion "Did you mean…through?" If you find the grammar checker catching phrases you use repeatedly, you can add them to the list of phrases just under the series of check boxes in the Proofreading option. For example, the proofreader often underlines the word *Technorama*, the title of one of the blogs I operate. Typing the word in the Ignored Phrases text field tells the proofreader not to underline the word, but to ignore it.

# Name

The following sections describe how to set or change your name and the way it is displayed to others (see Figure 2.2).

## Username

The Username is the name that you use for logging in to the system. It cannot be changed after it is set—not even by a user with Administrator rights.

## First Name, Last Name

The First Name and Last Name fields are used, of course, for your first name and last name (surname).

## Nickname

Your nickname can be different from your login name. It is the name that people will know you by. For example, I signed up with the account "ctomasi," but I want everyone to know me as "chucktomasi" on this blog. I can use the nickname to differentiate it from my login name. This capability is helpful because the login name cannot be changed.

## Display Name Publicly As

The value selected from the Display Name Publicly As list is how the system displays your name when you make a post. You can choose from your login name, nickname, first name only, last name only, or both in either order (see Figure 2.2). Changing this setting later updates any previous postings you have made. The system stores your real name with the posting and displays the value you select from the list.

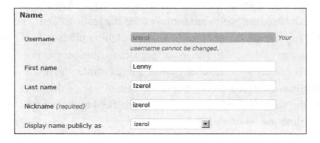

**FIGURE 2.2**    How the name part of the profile might be filled out.

# Contact Info

You use the Contact Info section to provide information regarding how other users can contact you. The only required field is E-mail, which is how WordPress contacts you when you have new comments or user registrations. WordPress automatically uses the email address you entered when you registered. If you try to change your email address here, WordPress puts your original email address back and sends a message to the new address you entered with a link that takes you to the settings where can make the actual change. The correct place to change your email address is in General Settings (explained in Lesson 4, "Configuring Your Blog Settings").

Optionally, you can provide your website, AOL Instant Messenger (AIM), Yahoo IM, and Jabber/Google Talk IDs for those who might want to reach you through one of those online services (see Figure 2.3).

**FIGURE 2.3** Provide additional contact information to let others know how to reach you.

# About Yourself

If you want to let your readers know a little bit more about you, fill in the About Yourself section. Although you aren't required to complete the fields in this section, sharing a bit of yourself with your readers is not a bad idea.

## Biographical Info

The text area labeled Biographical Info is a place for you to give a brief overview of yourself. The information you include here can be a simple one-line entry such as "Personality on the Technorama podcast," or it can be something a little more detailed. I recommend entering really in-depth personal information in the About page, which is explained in the "Completing Your About Page" section.

## New Password

At some point, you might need to change your password. If you host your own blog, you probably want to change your password right after you set up the blog with a default Administrator account and random password. Change your password in the section at the bottom of your profile.

Choosing a new password can be tricky. The goal is to use something meaningful that you are likely to remember, yet challenging enough so someone else won't be likely to guess it. Optimally, you don't want to use a password that has been used somewhere else in case that one has been compromised.

Here are a few guidelines for choosing a password:

- ▶ Use a password that is at least six characters long (the longer, the better).

- ▶ Use a combination of letters (upper- and lowercase), numbers, and symbols.

- ▶ Try to stay away from dictionary words.

- ▶ Use mnemonics (memory devices) to help you remember passwords.

- ▶ Change your password regularly. This procedure is a nuisance, but it's less painful than losing valuable data. Some people on the Internet seem to have nothing better to do than try to break into accounts on popular sites like WordPress.com.

WordPress offers a "strength indicator" just under the password field. As you type your password, WordPress tells you how good your password is on a rating from very weak to strong.

Examples of poor passwords are

- ▶ *wordpress*—All lowercase—too obvious.

- ▶ *1234abcd*—Although this example uses a combination of letters and numbers, it is fairly easy for a computer to calculate this combination.

- ▶ *Bunny*—Too short and uses a word from the dictionary.

Examples of strong passwords are

▶ *My1stBl0g!*— A decent length (10 characters); uses uppercase, lowercase, numbers, and symbols. Uses a mnemonic for "my first blog" to help you remember.

▶ *Ra!s!ns+Ch0c0late*—Although these look like dictionary words, symbols and numbers replace some letters, which makes it more difficult for a computer to crack but easy for a human to remember.

▶ *2Maps&2Chart$*—Uppercase, lowercase, numbers, symbols, and good length. Sometimes you only need to look around the room to find a good password.

# Your Gravatar

Gravatar is a concatenation of "global recognized" avatar. An avatar is a photo or other graphic that represents you. Avatars are usually 80 × 80 pixels in size. Normally, as you navigate around the Web, you need to upload an avatar to each site. A gravatar allows you to use one avatar across multiple sites, chat rooms, forums, and so on. You might see one in a WordPress site if the theme has been designed to display them.

There are several ways to set your WordPress gravatar. These include

▶ Uploading an existing image from your computer.

▶ Using your webcam to take a snapshot of yourself. You need a machine with a functioning webcam and Adobe FlashPlayer installed to take this approach.

▶ Using a link to an existing online image.

▶ Using your previous WordPress.com avatar (if you had one).

▶ Going to http://en.gravatar.com set your avatar there and having WordPress.com reference it.

This example uses an image from the local computer. The following steps walk you through one way of setting your gravatar:

1. Click on the image that looks like a sideways **G** in the upper right on your profile page (or the **Change Your Gravatar** link just below it). A window displays in front of the other text on your browser window (see Figure 2.4).

2. Click the link **Upload a New Image from Your Computer** to instruct WordPress to use an image on your computer as your gravatar.

3. Click the **Browse** button and look around for an image that suits you. When you have located an image, select it, click **Open**, and click the **Next** button.

4. The image file is sent to the server, and the gravatar image is displayed on the screen. A square on top of your image indicates the actual part of the image that is displayed (as shown in the two preview windows on the right).

5. Resize the box on top of your image by dragging the handlebars to change the size of the image area. You also can drag the square to a different area on your image.

6. After you have selected the appropriate area and your preview windows look the way you want, click the **Crop and Finish!** button.

7. Provide a rating for your image by clicking on the appropriate letter. Descriptions of the ratings are provided. Depending on the rating, your image may not be displayed on all sites that use gravatars.

8. Click the **X** in the upper right of the window to close the Gravatar window.

Your gravatar is associated with your email address; in this case, it's associated with the email address you provided for your WordPress.com account. If your gravatar does not appear right away, you might need to refresh your screen or click **Your Profile** (on the left).

Behind the scenes, you just interacted with the gravatar.com website to set your image across multiple websites.

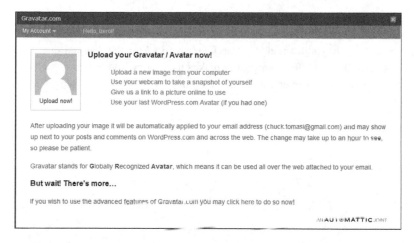

**FIGURE 2.4**  The screen for uploading your gravatar.

---

**Remember to Save Your Changes**

You must click the **Update Profile** button at the bottom of the page if you changed any options (excluding your gravatar). If you make changes and do not click Update Profile, your changes are lost.

---

# Completing Your About Page

Another way to tell your readers more about yourself is to set up a page with more detailed information than what is in your profile. WordPress presents a tip with a link at the top of the Dashboard like the one shown in Figure 2.5. If the tip is not available, use the side menu on the left, click the Pages section, then click About from the list of pages. You can find more information about creating and editing posts and pages in Lesson 3, "Creating Posts and Pages."

**FIGURE 2.5**  WordPress offers some useful tips on the Dashboard, such as this one about updating your About page.

# Summary

In this lesson, you learned to set up your profile. You also learned that setting preferences for your profile makes navigating and using WordPress.com more enjoyable and effective for you and your blog's readers.

# LESSON 3

# Creating Posts and Pages

*In this lesson, you learn how to create and manage posts and pages. This lesson introduces you to the basics of content creation and then more advanced topics such as including images, audio, and video to enrich your readers' experience.*

## Creating Posts

Posts are the lifeblood of any blog. They are the reason people come back to a blog or subscribe to an RSS feed. If a blog doesn't have an influx of new content, most people have no desire to visit. As a result, creating and maintaining posts are some of the most common activities you will perform on your site. Posts don't need to be fancy or laborious to create. The less time you spend thinking about how to operate the tool, the more time you can spend creating content. WordPress has provided several easy ways to create new posts.

The easiest way to create a new post is to click the **New Post** button in the upper-right corner of the administrative screen. You can always create a new post from the side menu under Posts, Add New. See Figure 3.1.

---

NOTE: **The New Post Button**
The New Post button is context sensitive, so it may not always appear as New Post.

---

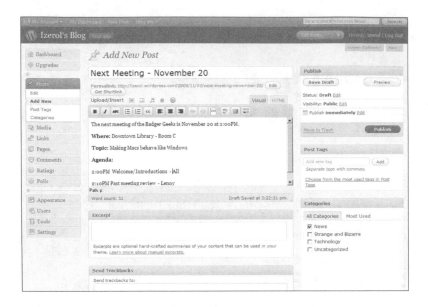

**FIGURE 3.1**   Adding a new post.

The first field at the top of the Add New Post page is the post title. This is the "headline" of your post. A good title is the key to a good post. It should grab the attention of your readers and draw them in. Often, it is the only part of your post some people will see, such as an RSS index listing.

After you finish entering your title and tab (or move your cursor) to the next field, a URL appears just below the title with the label Permalink. For now, this is the link to your post.

There are also two buttons below the title:

▶ **Edit**—This button allows you to modify the suffix of the URL. By default, WordPress creates the URL based on the date and the title words. Although you cannot change the date, you can change the part with the title words if you choose, as long as it remains unique. WordPress removes symbols such as $, &, and @ from the title to avoid confusion with special symbols used by web addresses. Use the **Edit** button next to the permalink to modify the URL. For example, add the word "percent" where WordPress removed the "%" symbol.

▶ **Short Link**—This button provides a quick way to take your
long URL and collapse it down to something easier to reference
in a short messaging system like a mobile text message or
Twitter. For example, your default permalink is http://your-
name.worpress.com/2009/11/27/funniest-bumper-stickers, and
the short link is http://wp.me/pGy8H-k.

At a minimum, all you need for a basic post is a title and text in the mes
sage body. Then click **Publish** and you've created a post! Of course, there
are many options to add more pizzazz to your posts. The following sections describe how to format and enhance your posts.

# The Visual Editor

Just below the title is the body of the post. This is the place where you
enter the text (and other items) of your post. This area operates much like
a standard word processor offering indentation, bullet lists, bold, italic,
centering, and other formatting options. More advanced content items are
covered later in this lesson. You can find out what each icon does by pass-
ing your cursor over it.

Consider, for example, that you want to write a quick review of *Sams
Teach Yourself WordPress in 10 Minutes*.

In the title area, enter **Book Review: Sams Teach Yourself WordPress in
10 Minutes**.

In the message body, begin typing some pertinent information, such as the
following:

```
Author: Chuck Tomasi and Kreg Steppe
Pages: 208
ISBN: 0672331209
Comments: Two thumbs up. "STY WordPress in 10 min" covers the
necessary information to get me up and running on WordPress.com
quickly and easily without a lot of extra "fluff" to get in the
way. The authors know their topic and stay on track. The informa-
tion is presented in a clear and logical order. I am new to
WordPress and I don't know a lot about online services and social
media, I had no trouble getting started with WordPress. I will
continue to use this as a reference should I need to host my own
blog (and customize it) in the future.
```

That's not too bad, but a little plain. Let's take a look at the Visual Editor toolbar and see how it might help us enhance our post. Some of the icons are covered later in this lesson to demonstrate how to include more than text in your post.

▶ When you highlight the word *Author* and click the **B** icon on the toolbar, the word turns bold. By repeating this procedure for the words *Pages*, *ISBN*, and *Comments*, you can enhance the look of your post by making the headers stand out.

▶ You might also highlight the title of the book and click the **I** icon to make the title italic. Don't go overboard with formatting, though.

▶ You can use the button that has the ABC with a line through to create "strikeout" text. Bloggers commonly use strikeout as a reminder to come back and update posts as new facts related to the topic emerge. By highlighting some text and clicking the strikeout icon, you leave the text in the post, but readers can see that it is obsolete.

▶ The icon to the right of strikeout lets you create a bulleted list. To create a new bulleted list, start with your cursor at the beginning of a new line and click the bullet list icon. A bullet appears, and you can begin typing your first list item. At the end of the first item, press **Enter** and a second bullet appears. Continue this process until you complete your list. When you are done, press **Enter** on a blank bullet (typically your last one), and your list is terminated. To create a bulleted list from existing text, highlight the lines where you want a bullet and click the bullet list icon.

▶ Numbered lists operate just like bullet lists. The icon for numbered lists is next to the bullet lists and has a 123 with lines next to it.

▶ The next three icons let you change the alignment of your text. For existing text, place the cursor on the line you want to align and click one of the icons to set it right-justified, centered, or left-justified. For new text, click the appropriate alignment icon first and then start typing. When you want to switch, choose a different icon and begin typing additional text.

▶ If you have a very long post, you might decide to use the More icon. This icon looks like a small white rectangle over a larger white rectangle with a dotted line between them. To use the More icon, place your cursor at a spot two or three lines into your post. For this example, place it right after ". . . get in the way." Now click the **More** icon, and you see a dividing line appear in your text. When readers view your post in their web browser, they will see the first couple of lines and then a link labeled Read the Rest of This Entry>>. If readers click the link, they are taken to a page with the entire post. This feature provides a good way for you to get lots of posts in a small space but still have the ability to be verbose.

▶ The button with the ABC and the check mark lets you spell check your posting. If WordPress finds an error, it underlines the error in red. Click the underlined word and several options are presented to allow you to correct or ignore the word.

▶ The second icon from the right toggles full-screen mode. If you prefer to temporarily clear your screen of everything that is not part of your post, you can click this icon to focus on your writing. Clicking it again goes back to the default view.

▶ The rightmost icon is known as the Show/Hide the Kitchen Sink button, which displays or hides an entire second row of icons. This button lets you change the font size, style, and color, as well as insert symbols, change your indent level, undo changes, and redo changes.

Be choosy about using enhancements in your post. Using too many can detract from the message you are trying to convey.

TIP: **Use Keyboard Shortcuts to Speed Up Your Work**

As you move your cursor over the icons on the Visual Editor toolbar, make a note of the text that appears when you hover over each one for a second or two. WordPress lets you know what keyboard shortcuts you can use to accomplish the same task without using your mouse. For example, hovering over the Bold icon displays (Ctrl+B). This means you can press B while holding down the Ctrl key, represented as Ctrl+B (Windows) (or ⌘-B for the Mac). Different browsers use different keys to access the shortcuts. You might have to hold down Alt+Shift instead of Ctrl. Rather than moving to the icon, clicking **B**, then typing text, and clicking the icon again, you can press Ctrl+B (to turn on bold), type your text, and press Ctrl+B again (to turn off bold). The more your hands stay on the keyboard, the faster you will become.

# WYSIWYG Editing Versus HTML

To the right of the Visual Editor toolbar are two tabs labeled Visual and HTML:

▶ **Visual**—This is the default option when you're creating posts. It allows you to create your post in a WYSIWYG (what you see is what you get) format common to most word processors today.

▶ **HTML**—Clicking this tab switches to show what is going on behind the scenes. It reveals the actual HTML codes necessary to display your text in a browser the way you intend (see Figure 3.2). Although you probably won't use the HTML window to enter the text of your posts (unless you are skilled with HTML), you might use the window to embed HTML code that you get from a third party.

**FIGURE 3.2**    The HTML tab lets you view see HTML code and insert HTML code from a third party.

# Using Excerpts, Trackbacks, and Discussion Options

Following the post message body on the screen is a text area labeled Excerpt. This optional bit of text gives a summary about your post. It is optional because it can be used to replace the full content in your RSS feed if you use the option to display summaries in Settings, Reading. And, depending on the WordPress theme used, you can use it where summaries are preferred to full content. These places include

- ▶ Search results

- ▶ Tag archives

- ▶ Category archives

- ▶ Monthly archives

- ▶ Author archives

The next section below Excerpt is Send Trackbacks. Trackbacks are a way to notify other blogs that you have linked to them, which is useful for getting not only your readers but also readers from another blog involved in the conversation. Trackbacks work like this:

- ▶ Person A writes something on her blog.

▶ Person B wants to comment on Person A's blog, but wants her own readers to see what she had to say, and be able to comment on her own blog.

▶ Person B posts on her own blog and sends a trackback to Person A's blog.

▶ Person A's blog receives the trackback and displays it as a comment to the original post. This comment contains a link to Person B's post.

If you link to other WordPress blogs, the trackback function is automatic, and you can leave it blank. For non-WordPress blogs, enter the URL of the other blog's post in the space provided.

Finally, in the main column are the Discussion options. They allow you to enable or disable comments and trackbacks on a post-by-post basis (over-riding the settings in the global discussion options in Settings, Discussion).

## Publish Options

The options in the Publish section on the right allow you to manage when and how your post is released to your readers.

▶ **Save Draft (button)**—The Save Draft button allows you to save your work as you continue writing. Few things are more frustrating than writing for a long time and then losing your work. Saving as a draft simply keeps a recent backup of your article on WordPress. Your content is saved but not yet published.

▶ **Preview (button)**—If you want to see how your post will look before it is made public, click the **Preview** button. A preview is useful when you have embedded images, additional formatting, or something else besides simple text and you want to verify the layout appears as you would expect.

▶ **Status (field)**—The Status defaults to Draft to indicate the post is under construction. You can click the **Edit** link next to the word *Draft* and change it to *Pending Review* if you want to have an editor review it before it is posted.

▶ **Visibility (field)**—The Visibility option allows you to change who can see your post. By default, it is set to Public, but by clicking the **Edit** link, you get several options, including password protected and private. Another handy feature under Visibility is the check box labeled Stick This Post to the Front Page. Some people like to use this option for announcements or other information they want to make available all the time. For example, if our local radio-controlled airplane club is having a monthly meeting in three weeks, I want that meeting announcement to stay on the front page even if there are a dozen more postings between the time I post the announcement and the meeting. Of course, I will have to remember to edit the article and uncheck that option at some point in the future.

▶ **Publish (field)**—You also can change the time the article is published. This capability is useful for dated material. For example, our local radio-controlled airplane club just got a pre-release of a new model to write a review. As part of the agreement, the review must be posted on the first of next month to coincide with the product release. When I click the **Edit** link next to Publish: Immediately, a date and time appear. I can set the date to the first of next month, determine what time it will show up, and click **OK**. After reviewing and setting all my options, I can click the **Publish** button.

▶ **Publish (button)**—The simplest action in this section is the Publish button. When you click it, your content is online for the world to read.

## Post Tags

Post tags provide a way to group similar post topics together in an informal way. When you create a post, you can add optional tags that work much like keywords. Posts with the same tags can be automatically linked together. Some WordPress themes display the tags to quickly access posts with the same tags. For example, my personal blog has a posting on it about my martial arts training. If I include tags such as *karate*, *training*, *exercise*, and *bo staff*, they are easily searchable among other WordPress.com blogs using the Dashboard, Tag Surfer feature. From an information organization standpoint, you should start getting in the habit of putting a few tags in each post. Post tags are managed from the side menu under Posts, Post Tags.

## Categories

Categories are another way to organize your information. They are more structured than post tags in that they can be hierarchical (one category can have one or more subcategories). When you create your blog, have a good idea of what types of information you will be sharing and create categories around the major groupings. For example, in my personal blog, I write about personal and professional topics. I further break down the personal topics into family, exercise, personal development, and hobbies. I have created my categories around these major groupings. When I create a post, I know it generally fits at least one of these categories. Before I publish the post, I can check the appropriate category (or categories). Now if someone comes to my blog and wants to see what I've written regarding my personal development program, he can click a category link (typically displayed on the front page of my blog under a Categories heading) and see those posts grouped together. Try not to go overboard on categories. Again, some forethought is recommended here.

> NOTE: **Using Tag Surfer**
> If you select the **Dashboard, Tag Surfer** option from the side menu, any tags you put in that list are automatically available to your post categories.

# Editing Existing Posts

Whether you've spotted a typo, need to make an update to a meeting agenda, or take something offline for legal reasons, you are going to need to make changes to your posts at some point. Editing existing posts is done by going to **Posts, Edit** in the side menu (see Figure 3.3).

**FIGURE 3.3**   A typical list of posts.

The Edit Posts list lets you see a number of properties about each post, including the author, any categories or tags applied, a quick link to statistics regarding your post, how many comments were made about it, and the date when it was last modified or published.

## List Basics

WordPress displays the index of posts, pages, comments, links, and media files in a list. Most lists in WordPress have the same basic functionality. Following is an overview of basic list operations:

▶ The column titles are available at the top and bottom of the list of articles for convenience when you're managing a long list of articles.

▶ Clicking **Screen Options** displays check boxes corresponding to the list column titles. Checking or unchecking turns on or off any of the columns in the listing after you click the **Apply** button.

▶ The Screen Options also allow you to control how many items are displayed in the list.

▶ Most lists have Add New near the top of the screen so that you can quickly add a new entry.

▶ Many lists have links that enable you to quickly view grouped items. For example, the Posts list has links labeled All, Published, Drafts, and Trash, enabling you to quickly view a subset of the entire list. The view for All items does not include those in the Trash.

▶ As you pass your cursor over any of the list items, notice the options that appear just under the title. They allow you to easily manage items. For example, on the Edit Posts list, placing the cursor anywhere on a row displays links labeled Edit, Quick Edit (see Figure 3.4), Trash, and View (or Preview for a draft).

▶ When you use the Trash link on a post, page, comment, or upload from your blog, it is not removed immediately. The Trash option moves it to the Trash folder, where it is still available for up to 30 days. WordPress.org users can configure the retention period by modifying their wp-config.php file. When you trash an item, an Undo link appears at the top of the list, allowing you to recall your trashed item immediately in case of an accident. Posts, pages, comments, and media each have their own Trash folder. To see items in the Trash folder, click the **Trash** link at the top of the list. Items in the Trash folder can be restored easily by placing your cursor over the item you want to restore and clicking the **Restore** link. Inversely, you can remove the file permanently by clicking the **Delete Permanently** link. The Links list uses a standard Delete link. After a link is deleted, it is permanently and immediately removed from the system. Previous versions of WordPress had a simple Delete feature that immediately removed items from the system.

▶ On the left of each list is a series of check boxes. Whether you are managing posts, users, or other list items, use these check boxes to select one or more items to perform a "bulk action" on them. Check the check box on the top or bottom title row to select all list items currently displayed. An example is approving comments en masse. You can either select all the comments one at a time or use the topmost (or bottommost) check box to check them all and then use the Bulk Actions drop-down list and click the **Apply** button to approve them all at once.

Other list options vary depending on specific functions to that list, such as filtering posts by categories. Don't be afraid to experiment with the list links.

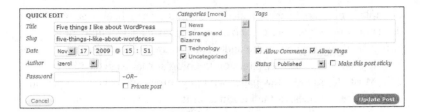

**FIGURE 3.4** Quick Edit allows you to edit nearly all post attributes from the edit list.

Other tools, specific to the Edit Posts listing, can be used to filter and modify the way your posts are displayed in the list. If you are extremely prolific and have hundreds of posts to sort through, you can try to find your material by using the filters just above the list column headings. They let you filter by certain dates and/or categories. Alternatively, you can use the search box to search for text in any of your posts.

You can also make edits on multiple posts by checking each entry and then use the Bulk Edit menu to select **Edit** and click **Apply**. A set of options appears at the top of the list similar to those found in the Quick Edit option. Using these options allows you to set categories, tags, the author, and other attributes on multiple posts at once.

Two additional icons appear at the top right of the Edit list to change the view from List view to Excerpt view. List view provides you with a concise list displaying just the article title. When you change to Excerpt view, you get a preview of posts just below the title. Some people find this feature useful, whereas others think it makes the list too long. You can choose which option you prefer. A sample of the Edit list is shown in Figure 3.3.

# Creating Pages

Pages contain static content that is quickly accessible from nearly anywhere on the blog, as opposed to a more dynamic influx of regular posts. As with posts, you can insert images, links, or any other type of information that the Visual Editor supports to create your page. One good

example is the About page (created by default). The About page is a
description of you or your organization. It gives readers a little more
background about who you are and what you are doing. Most themes
have a good way to display pages on the blog's front page (see Figure
3.5). Most blogs have a few pages with key information about the person,
organization, services, or the information it offers. You can arrange your
pages hierarchically with a parent page having multiple pages under it.
For example, your About page may also have pages with more detail on
your work history or hobbies.

**FIGURE 3.5**    This theme displays pages as tabs across the top.

## Creating Basic Pages

Creating a page is similar to creating a post. There are some differences
that I will point out as we walk through the process. To create a new page:

1. Click **Pages** from the side menu.

2. Click **Add New** from the Pages section.

3. Give your page a title. Keep your page title short (one or two
   words). Many themes display page titles horizontally. Short titles
   work much better in this situation.

4. Add the content. Page editing uses the same Visual Editor as the post editor, so all the same formatting tips described in the "Creating Posts" section also apply to pages.

5. Set the attributes. Unlike posts with tags and categories, pages have an Attributes section on the right. Defining the parent page allows you to arrange your pages hierarchically. For example, you may have a sporting goods products page that has "sub-pages" for hunting, fishing, tennis, and so on. All these pages would have the same parent page. The main page is the parent by default. The attributes section also has an option that allows you to define how your pages are ordered. If you leave all pages at 0, they are sorted alphabetically by title.

6. Set the comments and trackback options. Again, like posts, pages can allow comments and trackbacks (references) if the appropriate check boxes under the page body are checked.

7. Publish your post. The same options to publish your page (date, time, visibility, and so on) are also available.

## Editing Pages

Managing pages is similar to managing posts. Begin by selecting the **Pages** section in the side menu. A list of pages is presented (see Figure 3.6). Refer to the "List Basics" sidebar earlier in this lesson for the fundamentals of managing WordPress lists.

You can edit any page by clicking on the page name or using the **Edit** link that appears just below the title when your mouse cursor passes over the row containing the page information.

When the editor appears, change the title, content, or other options to suit your needs. You can find more information on the editor's features in the "Visual Editor" section earlier in this lesson. When you are done making changes, click **Update**.

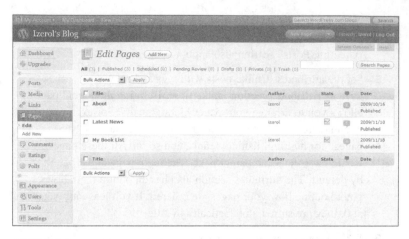

**FIGURE 3.6**    A typical page listing.

# Creating More Advanced Content

Creating basic text is nice, but WordPress is capable of so much more. What's more, web users these days expect references, images, and even audio and video from your site. WordPress has a way to accomplish all this without requiring you to know any web programming language.

## Adding Hyperlinks

Hyperlinks are references on a web page that, when clicked, take you to another location on the same page or to a different page altogether. Hyperlinks can either be text or an image. To place a hyperlink in your post or page (aka article), you first need to know the location of the other page. Follow these steps to add a text hyperlink:

1. Edit your article.

2. Open a second browser window or tab.

3. Go to the page you want to link to.

4. Select the text in the address bar. Be sure to get the entire address. Placing your cursor in the address bar usually highlights everything by default. However, if you don't have everything

selected, you can press Ctrl+A (Windows)/⌘-A (Mac) to select all text.

5. Right-click your mouse and select **Copy** or press Ctrl+C (Windows)/⌘-C (Mac).

6. Close the second browser window or tab.

7. In the Visual Editor, use your cursor to select the text you want to use as your link.

8. Click the icon that looks like two links of a chain.

9. The Insert/Edit Link window displays with several fields (see Figure 3.7). Fill in the fields as follows:

    ▶ **Link URL**—This is the address you copied from the address bar in the other window. Type or paste the complete web address by pressing Ctrl+V (Windows)/⌘-V (Mac).

    ▶ **Target**—This identifies where the new page will be displayed.

    ▶ **Title**—The text in the title is what pops up when you move your cursor over the link. Many times it is the same as the text of the link, but can be different. For example, the text might contain "Chuck Tomasi" and the title contains "Chuck's home page."

    ▶ **Class**—The class identifies the style in which the link is displayed. The values in this field refer to the cascading style sheet (CSS) values. CSS is beyond the scope of this book. It's OK to leave the class with the default value "—Not Set—".

10. Click **Insert**.

**FIGURE 3.7**    You only need to know the URL to create a hyperlink.

---

TIP: **Check All Your Links**

Be sure to verify your links connect with the pages you intend by testing them. If you need to correct your link, place your cursor anywhere on the linked text and click the **Link** icon.

---

## Adding Images

Adding images to your article communicates much more information than text alone. Inserting images into your article is available four ways:

1. From your computer

2. From a URL (another website)

3. From the gallery (available after images are uploaded)

4. From the media library

Begin any of these methods by placing your cursor in the body of your text where you want to insert the image and then click the **Add an Image** icon (see Figure 3.8). The Add an Image window opens (see Figure 3.9).

### Adding an Image From Your Computer

To add an image from your computer, follow these steps:

1. Select the left option (**From Computer**) at the top of the Add an Image window. You can upload JPEG, GIF, or PNG image files by clicking the **Select Files** button.

**2.** Use your computer's browse feature to select the file(s) you want to upload.

**3.** Click **Open** (Windows) or **Select** (Mac). Your file is uploaded, and a thumbnail of your image is displayed with various properties.

**4.** Click the **Insert Into Post** button. Use the scroll bar on the Add an Image window to look further down if you don't see the button displayed.

The Add an Image icon

**FIGURE 3.8**   Use the Add an Image icon to include photos, icons, and other graphics.

Your image is then inserted into your post. If you need to modify any of the image properties, such as alignment, size, caption, and so on, click your image and two icons appear in the upper-left corner of your image. Click the icon that looks like a mountain and sky to edit your image; click the red circle with a slash through it to delete your image.

**FIGURE 3.9**    Images can be added to your article several ways.

---

TIP: **Add Alternate Text for Accessibility**

When you add images, consider using the Alternate Text field to describe your image. Alternate text can be used for visually impaired readers who use special software that scans for the text in Alternate Text fields and reads it audibly. When you upload an image, the Alternate Text field is listed below the Title. When you edit your image, the field is listed under the Advanced Settings tab.

---

NOTE: **How Many Images Can I Use?**

You can upload up to 3GB of files before requiring a storage upgrade.

---

## Adding an Image From a URL

Another way to add an image to your article is to reference it from another location (someone else's site) or add it by using the URL. Adding an image by using a URL saves you disk space and ensures changes to an image at the source are reflected on your site. The downside is that your site is generating traffic on the other server instead of your own server, which is sometimes frowned upon. Another disadvantage is the lack of control you have on the image you are using. If someone on the other site deletes the file, you will find yourself with a missing image. Before you use this option, be sure you have permission to include images through the URL. To add an image from a URL, do the following:

1. Determine the URL to the image you want to use by going to that page and right-clicking on the image.

2. Copy the URL. Depending on your browser:

   ▶ Firefox: Choose Copy Image Location.

   ▶ Internet Explorer. Choose Properties and copy the text from the Address (URL) field.

   ▶ Safari: Choose Copy Image Address.

3. Click the **Add an Image** icon from the toolbar.

4. In the Add an Image window (see Figure 3.10), click the **From URL** tab.

5. Copy the the Image URL by placing your cursor in the Image URL field and typing Ctr+V (Windows), ⌘-V (Mac), or right-click and choose Paste.

6. Add descriptive text to the Alternate Text field.

7. Enter a caption (optional).

8. Specify how you want the image aligned (optional).

9. If you want the image to link to another site or page when the reader clicks on the image, enter the URL in the Link Image To field (this field is blank by default).

10. Click the **Insert Into Post** button at the bottom.

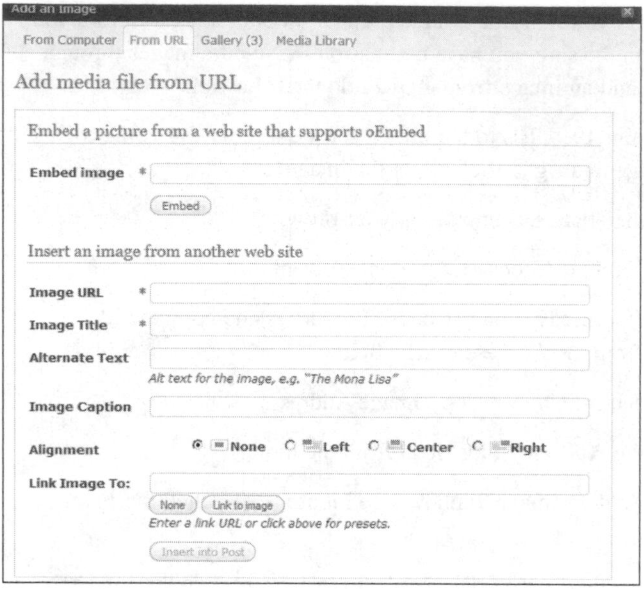

**FIGURE 3.10** Referencing media from another site.

Your image is now part of your article. To edit the image properties, click the image and then click the icon that looks like a mountain and sky that appears in the upper-left corner.

When the Add an Image window appears, notice that there is a second way to insert an image by using a URL (refer to Figure 3.10). The option at the top uses a protocol known as *oEmbed*. Without getting too technical, oEmbed is a new technology to address some problems discovered with referencing media from another site with a direct URL. The advantage of oEmbed is that it provides additional information about the media being requested so that the software (WordPress in this case) can be smarter about how it is embedded. The capability to embed an image is supported by many popular media sites such as YouTube, Flickr, and Hulu; more are being added all the time. For more information about oEmbed, visit www.oembed.com.

### Adding an Image from the Gallery

Your gallery is a collection of images attached to a post or page. It is a subset of the media library (a collection of all images and media files uploaded to your blog). When you add another image to the same article, a fourth option labeled Gallery appears on the top of the Add an Image window (see Figure 3.11). This option enables you to view the images attached to that article and insert them as a collection in the post.

For example, let's say I have several images from my summer vacation. Rather than inserting the images individually to the post or page, I can create a gallery using the following steps:

1. Click the **Add an Image** icon.

2. Click the From Computer tab to upload the images the same as you would to insert the images in to a post.

3. Instead of clicking **Insert into Post**, click **Save All Changes**.

4. Click the **Insert Gallery** button to add all four images at once.

Changing the settings of your gallery is similar to images. Click on the gallery after it is added to your post or page and use the upper-left icon to change where the image thumbnails link to, the order of the images, and how many columns to display. Click **Update Gallery Settings** to save your changes. You can find additional information about the Gallery at http://en.support.wordpress.com/images/gallery/.

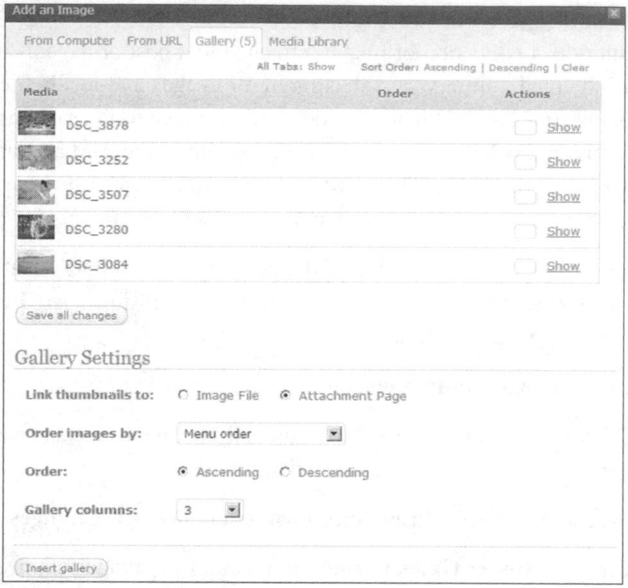

**FIGURE 3.11** The Gallery tab lets you insert a collection of images.

NOTE: **The Difference Between the Media Library and Gallery**

The media library is a warehouse of images, audio, video, and other files you can include in any post or page. The gallery is a collection of images specific to the current post or page.

### Adding an Image From The Media Library

The final way to add an image to your article is from your media library. After you load images into your media library, you can easily add images to an article:

1. Click the cursor where you want to insert the graphic in your text.

2. Click the **Add an Image** icon from the toolbar.

3. When the Add an Image window appears, click **Media Library** at the top.

4. Locate the image you want to include using the Search or Filter options.

5. After you locate the image, click the **Show** link on the right side.

6. Enter the title, alternate text, and other fields to format the image the way you like.

7. Click the **Insert Into Post** button at the bottom

Your image is then included as part of your article. The benefit of using images from your library is they can be used multiple times from one copy. This capability can save you time if you use a logo in multiple places. Updating your logo in the library updates it everywhere automatically. Also, you control what is in your media library, unlike referencing an image from another site.

NOTE: **Image Links**

By default, images uploaded from your system and those from the media library link to a full-size image of the one displayed in your article. That is, when readers click the image in your post or page, they go to a full-size version of your image. To change this, edit the properties and set the Link URL field to the address you want to link to.

## Adding Audio

Adding audio to your blog can turn your readers into listeners. There is something more intimate about hearing someone's voice than reading her words. Some bloggers have combined blogging with audio production to create a new media form called *podcasting*. Podcasting is beyond the scope of this book, but you can learn more about it in *Podcasting For Dummies*, Second Edition, by Tee Morris, Chuck Tomasi, and Evo Terra.

There are three ways you can include audio in your blog. The first is to upload an MP3 file somewhere on the Internet and insert a "short code" to use the built-in audio player in WordPress to play the file. (Creating and

uploading the MP3 file are beyond the scope of this book.) If you have a
file you want to reference and know the URL, you can do the following:

1. Edit your article.

2. Switch the Visual Editor to HTML mode by clicking the **HTML**
   link above the text edit box.

3. Enter the short code in the format: [audio
   http://mydomain.com/audio/myfile.mp3], replacing the URL
   with your appropriate address.

4. Save your article.

Your article then has a simple embedded audio player that visitors to your
site can click and hear.

The second way to include audio in an article is to buy the space upgrade
from WordPress (available under Dashboard, Upgrades) to enable uploading of audio files to your media library. From the Visual Editor, you can
also use the **Add Audio** icon (shaped like musical notes). Audio files supported are WAV, MP3, MP4, M4A, and OGG. After you purchase the
upgrade, the process of uploading and managing audio files is similar to
managing images.

The final way you can add audio to a post is to create a link that references your file elsewhere on the Internet. This requires your readers to
download the file and play it on their machine.

---

CAUTION: **Be Aware of Copyrights**

Whenever you're dealing with audio and video, be sure you understand and respect copyright laws associated with the material you
are using. When in doubt, do not use other people's work.

---

## Adding Video

High-speed Internet access is becoming more common every day. People are turning to the Internet for video to satisfy their entertainment and educational desires.

The first way you can embed a video from another site is to use the same method as linking an image from a URL. As with images, you need to know the URL of the video you are linking to. Most YouTube videos display the URL on the right side of the screen when you play it, so adding them is simply a matter of copying and pasting the URL from one window to another.

1. Open your article for editing.

2. Click the **Add Video** icon (shaped like a frame of a movie reel, to the right of the Add Image icon).

3. Click the **From URL** tab on the Add Video screen.

4. Enter the video URL—for example,
   `http://www.youtube.com/watch?v=sC0l06_223I`.

5. Click **Insert into Post**.

The second way you can include video is to purchase the VideoPress upgrade from WordPress (available under Dashboard, Upgrades) to upload and host your own video files in the media library. Uploading files can be done either from Media, Add New, or using the Add Video icon above the Visual Editor when you edit your article. Uploading or selecting the video from the media library follows the same steps you use with images. After you upload or select from the media library, the screen to define the attributes is a bit different (see Figure 3.12), allowing you to set a title, description, and rating. The selection also shows a short code you can use to embed the video, or you can click the **Insert into Post** button to include the video.

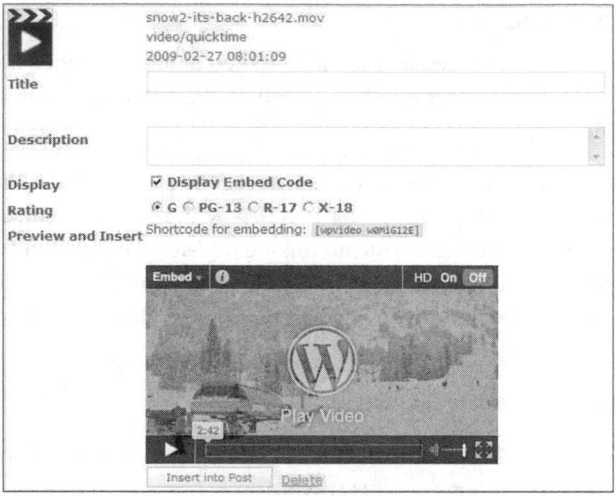

**FIGURE 3.12** Setting the options on an embedded video.

The advantage to putting your video on a site like YouTube is that it is free. The disadvantages are that videos are limited to 10 minutes or less, and if you ever want to produce content as part of a business, YouTube does not offer some of the controls and statistics you may need. To address those needs, you might want to consider the VideoPress upgrade.

# Summary

Adding new content is a common activity for bloggers. WordPress makes it easy to access the buttons and links to create posts and pages. The less time you spend focusing on how to use the tool, the more time you can spend on creating the content. Finally, your content can be enhanced by using some formatting, images, audio, and video to provide richer content and attract more visitors to your site.

# Configuring Your Blog Settings

*In this lesson, you learn the various options to configure the global settings on your blog to determine how people and other systems use it.*

Before you start creating content, it pays to ensure you have your blog configured to best meet your needs and those of your visitors. The information you entered when you set up your account was a good start, but there is more. Many of the default settings work fine, but in some cases customizing settings can help you and your readers use the system more effectively. The system settings control how the system behaves for everyone who uses it—from the way the time and date are displayed to the way you are notified when a comment is made.

The Settings section on the side menu is your key to configuring your system and the way people interact with it. The system settings are subdivided into General, Writing, Reading, Discussion, Media, Privacy, Delete Blog, OpenID, and Domains. Each of these subpanels is described in greater detail in this lesson.

## General

The General subpanel contains many of the settings related to the blog and some of the general interface properties (see Figure 4.1). The nine settings in the General subpanel are described in the following sections.

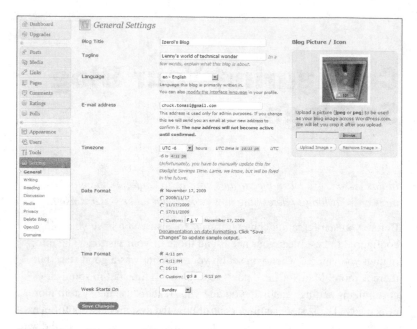

**FIGURE 4.1**    The General Settings screen.

# Blog Title

The Blog Title setting shows the title of your blog as it appears to others who are searching for or subscribing to it. Examples include "Valley Fair Orchestra," "Dean's Car Blog," and "Gmail Podcast."

# Tagline

The tagline is a short one-line description that lets people know what your blog is about. For example, one of my blogs is about Gmail and has the tagline "A collection of short hints, tips, and tricks to help you get more from your Gmail Account."

# Language

In the Language field, select the language the blog is written in. The default language is English. Note that this is different from the interface language readers may have set in their profiles.

# E-mail Address

The email address listed in the General Settings subpanel is for administrative purposes only and is not visible to your visitors. For example, it is the email address to which notifications are sent when new comments need to be approved. When you change the email address, a verification message is sent to the new address to confirm it for security reasons. The new email address is not active until the verification is complete.

# Timezone

The Timezone setting controls the display of times on the blog (such as when posts were made). The Timezone setting shows the current coordinated universal time, or UTC. You can change the Timezone setting to the offset of your timezone to UTC. Unfortunately, you have to manually adjust for daylight saving time. If you do not know the correct offset, you can use the UTC and sample current time to determine the proper value.

# Date Format

The Date Format setting lets you choose how to display dates in your blog. Alternatively, you can create your own custom format using the WordPress defined date codes. Documentation on the date codes is available just below the custom date format option.

# Time Format

The Time Format field allows you to choose how the time is displayed in your blog. You can choose 12-hour, 24-hour, or another variation with the custom setting.

# Week Starts On

WordPress recognizes that not everyone considers Sunday the first day of the week, so it offers the Week Starts On option, which allows you to start your calendar on any day of the week. Typically, this is Sunday or Monday, but you can use any value if your situation requires it.

## Blog Picture/Icon

The Blog Picture/Icon area shows the icon or the blavatar (short for blog avatar) of your blog. When people see references to your blog on WordPress.com, they see this image. To upload a new image, follow these steps:

1. Click the **Browse** button.

2. Select a JPG or PNG format image file from your system and click **OK**.

3. Click **Upload Image**.

4. Crop the image by resizing the dotted line cutout template and clicking **Crop Image**.

5. Click **Back to Blog Options**.

---

CAUTION: **Make Sure to Save**

If you have changed any of the General settings, be sure to click **Save Changes** at the bottom of the screen to ensure your changes take effect.

---

# Writing

The settings in the Writing subpanel apply to everyone who has permission to create content (posts and pages) on your system. These settings define how the authoring process actually works. See Figure 4.2 for the settings in the Writing subpanel.

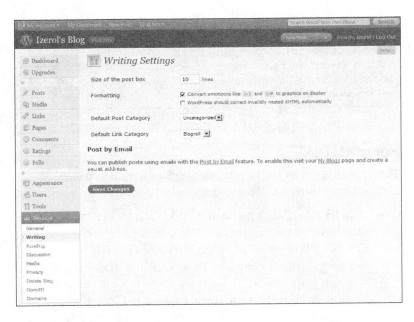

**FIGURE 4.2** The Writing Settings screen.

# Size of the Post Box

When you create a new post or page, a text box with tool icons is used to compose your content. This is known as the Visual Editor. To control the number of rows the Visual Editor text area displays, you can change the Size of the Post Box setting on this screen. You are not limited to only the number of lines of text specified with this setting; instead, after you've exceeded the number of lines of text the text box can accommodate, a scroll bar appears on the side of the text box. If you use a Netbook (small form-factor laptop) with limited vertical resolution, you might want to set this value lower so the text box fits on the screen. If you have a higher-resolution screen, you may choose to increase this value so you can get a better idea of what your completed work looks like.

CAUTION: **Be Aware of Coauthors' Limitations**

The Size of the Post Box setting is for all content contributors on the system. Even if you have a high-resolution screen and set the number of lines to 40, that may not work well if one of your editors uses a Netbook to create posts.

# Formatting

The Formatting option currently has two settings to help automate some of the content you create. These settings are

▶ **Convert Emoticons Like :-) and :-P to Graphics on Display—** Many people like to express emotion in their posts with symbols such as :-). When these characters are viewed sideways, they represent a smile or happiness. These symbols are affectionately known as *emoticons*. There are many others that can be used to enhance a potentially sterile communication or clear up writing that might be interpreted incorrectly. When you enable this option in WordPress, the software automatically recognizes key symbol sequences and replaces them with an appropriate small graphics (turning the smile the right side up, for example), making it easier for the readers.

▶ **WordPress Should Correct Invalidly Nested XHTML Automatically—**This option is useful for people who create their posts and pages using the HTML tab on the Visual Editor instead of using the graphical interface. For example, rather than change a font size with the icon from the Visual Editor toolbar, they use XHTML code. If you use the graphical interface of the Visual Editor or are really good at writing XHTML, you can leave this option turned off. You might consider turning it on if you are a casual XHTML writer who could use some assistance to avoid some possible aesthetic, and potentially catastrophic, issues with your system.

PLAIN ENGLISH: **XHTML**

XHTML stands for Extensible Hypertext Markup Language. This is the language web pages are written in and how WordPress ultimately presents content to your browser. It is possible to use WordPress to create XHTML directly, or flip between graphical and XHTML modes in the Visual Editor. In some cases, you may find it necessary to insert XHTML code directly in to your content.

# Default Post Category

When you create a new post, you have the option of selecting one or more categories. The Default Post Category setting allows you to have one category automatically selected. By default, it is set to Uncategorized. More information on categories is presented later in this lesson.

# Default Link Category

Links, typically displayed on a blog's (front page) sidebar, can be categorized like posts. When you create a new link, the Default Link Category setting determines the default category, possibly saving you a mouse click. The default value is Blogroll.

# Post by Email

It is possible to set up WordPress to allow content to be published simply by emailing it to a "secret" address. To set up Post by Email, refer to the section "Email Posting with WordPress.com" in Lesson 12.

NOTE: **Post by Email Formatting**

To use Post by Email, you need to use a mail client that supports rich text formatting or HTML content. Most desktop clients today have this capability.

When you use Post by Email, WordPress retains as much formatting as possible. Single images are placed inline with your text. For more information and details about formatting, visit http://en.support.wordpress.com/post-by-email/.

---

CAUTION: **Make Sure to Save**

If you have changed any of the Writing settings, be sure to click **Save Changes** at the bottom of the screen to ensure your changes take effect.

---

# Reading

The Reading options control how your posts and pages are presented to readers who receive your content via a web page and through an RSS feed. See Figure 4.3.

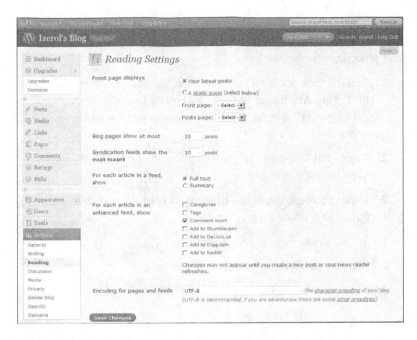

**FIGURE 4.3** The Reading Settings screen controls how posts are displayed on your web page and RSS feed.

# Front Page Displays

The Front Page Displays setting determines what is displayed on the front page when people first visit your blog. By default, they see your latest posts. This is the default setting because most readers like to see the latest information when they come to visit.

Alternatively, you can configure WordPress to show a static page on the front screen. Selecting A Static Page option and defining a specific page gives your site a more commercial feel with information about you or your organization on the front page. The second option, Posts Page, lets you configure how people find your posts if you are using a static front page. Refer to Lesson 3, "Creating Posts and Pages," for information on creating and maintaining pages. Here is an example of how the front page and posts pages are set up:

1.  Create a page about you or your organization. You can modify the default About page or create a new one by going to **Pages**, **Add New**. Fill in or modify the title and content to suit your needs.

2.  Create and save a second page with the title **Latest News** and leave the page body blank.

3.  Under **Settings**, **Reading**, change the **Front Page Displays** option to **A Static Page**.

4.  Set the **Front Page** to your About page.

5.  Set the **Posts Page** to your Latest News page.

6.  Click **Save Changes**.

Now when you view your site, your About information is displayed on the front, and a link to the Latest News containing all your posts is listed with the other pages.

---

CAUTION: **Using the Front Page Option**

If you set the Front Page option to one of your available pages and leave the Posts Page option as -Select-, readers might not be able to find your posts unless you have the Archives widget available. Refer to Lesson 6, "Personalizing the Appearance of Your Blog," for more information about widgets.

---

# Blog Pages Show at Most

As people are reading through your posts from your blog page or archives, you have the option to display as many or as few posts as you like. The default for the Blog Pages Show at Most option is 10. Depending on the average length of your posts, you might want to make this number higher if you have lots of short postings, or lower if your posts are more lengthy.

## Syndication Feeds Show the Most Recent

Using the Syndication Feeds Show the Most Recent setting, similar to the preceding setting, you can control how many posts are available in your RSS feed. The more posts you send, the more people have to download and potentially catch up on reading.

## For Each Article in a Feed, Show

For your RSS feed, you can send out a summary (the first 55 words) or the full text of your article by changing the For Each Article in a Feed, Show setting. Summaries are useful if readers have limited bandwidth. However, they force the readers to click something for the full content if they find your information useful. Some bloggers prefer to send the full text so the readers have the entire post at their fingertips.

## For Each Article in an Enhanced Feed, Show

You can choose to enhance your feed by including categories, tags, comment count, and some social web links. You do so by altering the For Each Article in an Enhanced Feed, Show setting. These are all option fields, and they may generate interest if your readers want to inform others or interact with you a little easier.

## Encoding for Pages and Feeds

Encoding lets you change the character encoding you write your blog in. There are many options to choose from. Unless you are certain you need to change the Encoding for Pages and Feeds setting, leave it at the default value (UTF-8).

# Discussion

One of the advantages of blogging over traditional media (magazines, newspapers, and so on) is the ability to interact and provide instant feedback to what you read and see. On the Discussion subpanel (see Figure 4.4)

of the Settings, you can configure how people and other blogs interact
with you.

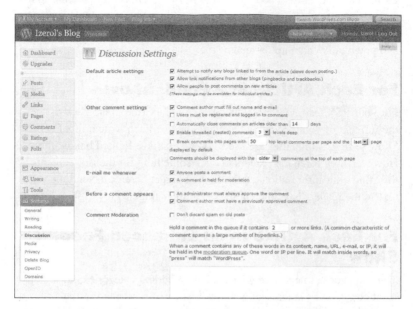

**FIGURE 4.4**   Part of the Discussion Settings options that determine how
comments, notifications, and avatars are handled.

# Default Article Settings

The three settings in Default Article Settings determine the default settings for new posts and pages. They can be overwritten individually per
article. The first two options deal with communicating between blogs
when one blog references another. Notification between sites is a great
way to see who is talking about you and, in turn, letting other bloggers
know you are talking about them.

# Other Comment Settings

The Other Comment Settings section controls how visitors create comments and how comments are displayed. The settings include

- ► **Comment Author Must Fill Out Name and E-mail**—This setting determines if people leaving comments are required to leave their names and valid email addresses (the option is checked) or can leave anonymous comments (the option is unchecked).

- ► **Users Must Be Registered and Logged In to Comment**—You can limit your comments to only registered WordPress.com users by checking this option. If you leave it unchecked, any visitor is allowed to make a comment.

- ► **Automatically Close Comments on Articles Older Than __ Days**—This setting allows you limit the number of days you are willing to accept comments on an article after it is published. After the number of days has elapsed, comments are no longer accepted. This feature is useful to mitigate spam attacks. It is common for spammers to continue to attack an old post after they discover it.

- ► **Enable Threaded (Nested) Comments __ Levels Deep**—Turn on this option to allow visitors to reply to other comments inline/nested. When turned on, it can allow for better discussions and responses. Standard convention uses a maximum of three levels deep; anything higher and the theme layouts may not work as expected.

- ► **Break Comments into Pages with __ Comments per Page and the __ Last Page Displayed by Default**—If your posts/pages get a lot of comments, you may want to split the comments into pages. You can choose how many top-level comments to show for each page. You can also choose which page to show by default when a visitor first views the comments.

- ► **Comments Should Be Displayed with the __ Comments at the Top of Each Page**—This setting allows you to display your comments oldest to newest or put the newest at the top.

## E-mail Me Whenever

The E-mail Me Whenever section contains two options. The first, Anyone Posts a Comment, notifies the author when comments are made to a post. If you check the second, A Comment Is Held for Moderation, an email is sent to the address you set in the General settings. If you leave this option unchecked, you can moderate your comments from the Dashboard or Comments.

## Before a Comment Appears

The Before a Comment Appears settings control how comments appear on the blog. When checked, the first option requires all comments to be approved by an administrator. The second option allows people who have made previously approved comments to bypass any further approvals.

## Comment Moderation

The Comment Moderation setting allows you to further refine moderated comments. You can opt to discard spam on old posts; hold comments if they contain a large number of links (a common spam characteristic); or identify key words, phrases, or addresses that might appear in a spam comment. This option does not mark the comment as spam, only that it needs to be moderated.

## Comment Blacklist

Similar to the preceding option, the Comment Blacklist setting allows you to identify spam comments by key words, phrases, or addresses that appear in the contents.

## Comment Reply via Email

The Comment Reply via Email option allows you to reply to comments right from the notification email. You need to enable Email Me Whenever: Anyone Posts a Comment to be able to reply to comments via email.

# Subscribe to Comments

The label Subscribe to Comments has one option that reads Don't Allow
Visitors to Subscribe to the Comments Made on This Blog. When this
option is unchecked, readers are provided a checkbox option at the bottom
of the comment section marked Notify Me of Follow-up Comments via
Email. If the reader checks this option, she is sent an email message
whenever someone else makes a comment on the same blog item. The
person commenting does not have to have a WordPress.com login to leave
comments or receive notifications. The email address the reader provides
is used to send the notifications. If Subscribe to Comments is checked, the
option to receive follow-up notifications is not presented.

# Avatars

Avatars are the icons that represent people in the virtual world. This section defines how you wish to display avatars on your blog.

- ▶ **Avatar Display**—This setting determines if avatars are displayed next to comments.

- ▶ **Maximum Rating**—When people create their avatars, they give
ratings to them similar to movie ratings. This option allows you
to filter avatars beyond a certain rating.

- ▶ **Default Avatar**—For users without a defined avatar, you can
choose to display a default (static) avatar or a custom one generated based on their email address.

> CAUTION: **Make Sure to Save**
> If you have changed any of the Discussion settings, be sure to click
> **Save Changes** at the bottom of the screen to ensure your changes
> take effect.

# Media

The Media settings allow you to override the default WordPress settings for image sizes in your blog (see Figure 4.5). This capability gives you some flexibility on the size of images to work better with your theme. All image sizes are specified in pixels and keep the dimension proportions (so they won't look squashed) to the maximum height or width. For example, specifying 300×300 won't force a 1600×1200 image to be square; it is converted to 300×225.

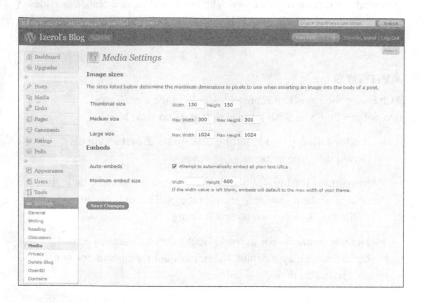

**FIGURE 4.5** The Media Settings screen lets you control how embedded content is displayed.

# Image Sizes

The following three settings indicate the maximum image size in pixels when you insert an image into a page or post.

> ▶ **Thumbnail Size**—This option specifies the size of the thumbnail images that are displayed as a preview of your images. Images are cropped and resized to fit the dimensions you set.

▶ **Medium Size**—This option sets the maximum size for an inline image in your post or gallery.

▶ **Large Size**—This option sets the maximum size of an image in your gallery, typically on its own page, free from the constraints your theme may impose.

## Embeds

The following two Embed options enable you to control how embedded content (typically video) is displayed on your blog:

▶ **Auto-Embeds**—If this option is checked, WordPress attempts to convert plain URLs to embedded content. This makes it quite simple to place YouTube videos on your site, for example.

▶ **Maximum Embed Size**—This option lets you specify the maximum height and width of your embedded content. This capability helps keep the site clean when you have a theme with a narrow column for your posts and you try to embed a wide video. If you leave the width column blank, embedded content defaults to the width specified by your theme.

# Privacy

Privacy settings control who can find and read your blog. They are accessed from the Privacy subpanel under Settings (see Figure 4.6) These settings are different from the privacy settings on individual posts discussed in Lesson 3. The three options for entire blog privacy are

▶ **I Would Like My Blog to Be Visible to Everyone, Including Search Engines (Like Google, Sphere, Technorati) and Archivers**—This is the default option. It indicates that your blog is open to the public.

▶ **I Would Like to Block Search Engines, but Allow Normal Visitors**—This option allows human visitors but prevents search engines from finding and indexing your information.

▶ **I Would Like My Blog to Be Visible Only to Users I Choose**—
Using this option, you can add and remove up to 35 users who
have access to your blog. Users must have registered
WordPress.com accounts. Upgrades are available if you require
more than 35 private users on your blog.

---

NOTE: **Privacy Is Not Absolute**

WordPress.com employees can read any blog regardless of privacy
settings.

---

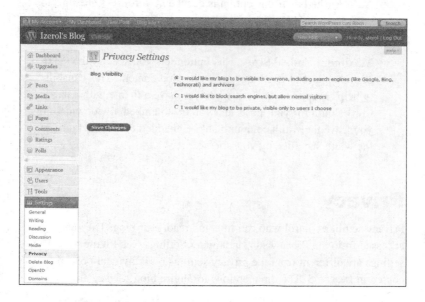

**FIGURE 4.6**   The Privacy Settings screen.

# Delete Blog

The Delete Blog option lets you delete your blog from WordPress.com.
Blog deletion requires confirmation. When you delete a blog, it is gone
forever. There may be a time when you no longer maintain your blog or

have so many that one becomes obsolete, and this is your option to remove it. Even after you delete a blog, that WordPress domain name can no longer be used.

# OpenID

OpenID is an open standard that allows you to sign in to sites using your WordPress.com account. Your OpenID is your blog URL (for example, http://myblog.wordpress.com). You can maintain the list of blogs that you trust and can use your OpenID as a login by adding it to the list in the OpenID section under Settings.

---

CAUTION: **OpenID Is Specific to a Site, Not a Person**

Anyone with an administrator account on your blog has access to your OpenID. Granted, you should already trust your administrators.

---

Other sites that use OpenID can be found at www.myopenid.com/directory.

# Domains

The Settings, Domains page is identical to the Upgrades, Domains page. On this page you can make changes to any mapped domain you own. You can map your WordPress.com domain (for example, example.wordpress. com) to any domain you own (such as example.com) so users think they are going to your domain and end up at your blog. If you ever plan to host your own WordPress blog at some point in the future, you should consider paying for the domain mapping service.

# Summary

The general settings control the global behaviors of your blog. How people and other blogs interact with your system is up to you to control.

# LESSON 5
# Managing Comments

*In this lesson, you learn what comments are, whether to allow them, and if you allow them, some best practices for managing your feedback.*

## Understanding Comments

One of the most exciting aspects of blogging is receiving comments. Comments are a way for your readers to interact with you, the author. They give your readers a way to provide feedback to you. Comments also allow readers to interact with each other.

When you first publish an article (a post or a page), it might have a 0 Comments or Leave a Comment link at the top or bottom of the post (depending on your theme). See Figure 5.1.

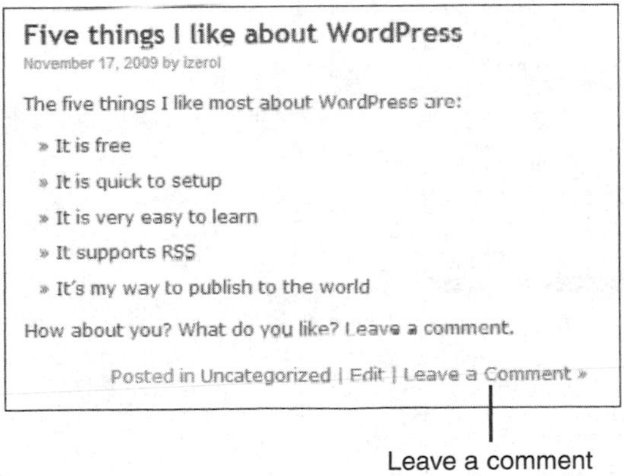

---

**Five things I like about WordPress**
November 17, 2009 by lzerol

The five things I like most about WordPress are:

» It is free
» It is quick to setup
» It is very easy to learn
» It supports RSS
» It's my way to publish to the world

How about you? What do you like? Leave a comment.

Posted in Uncategorized | Edit | Leave a Comment »

---

Leave a comment

**FIGURE 5.1**   WordPress makes it easy for readers to leave comments for you.

To leave a comment, the reader simply clicks the Leave a Comment link.
The page of multiple posts is replaced with a page displaying the entire
content of the specific post about which the reader is commenting. Text
input boxes for the reader to leave a comment are at the bottom of the page.
If you have comments enabled, one of two different options is displayed.

If readers are not already logged in to WordPress (which most won't be),
several fields appear requesting the following information (see Figure 5.2):

▶ **Name (required)**—This is the reader's name. Readers can use
real names, nicknames, or handles to identify themselves.

▶ **Email (required)**—Readers need to identify themselves to
WordPress in the event that they need to be notified later. Email
addresses are not displayed publicly.

▶ **Website (optional)**—If readers have websites and want to enter
the addresses, their names are displayed as hyperlinks so anyone
clicking on their name is directed to their site.

▶ **Comment text area**—This is the place where readers leave their
feedback to you, the author.

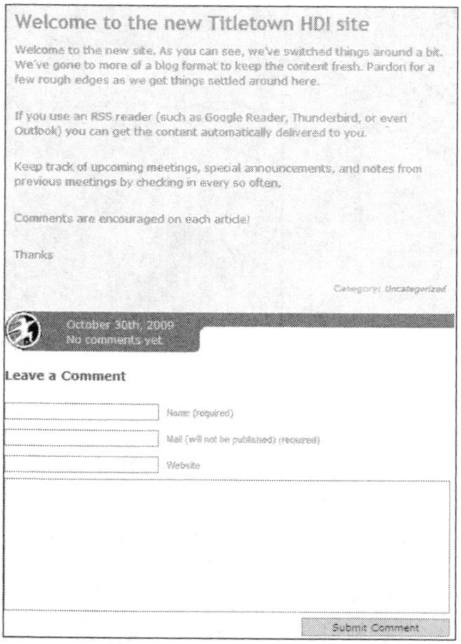

**FIGURE 5.2** Readers need to leave their name and email if they are not
already logged in.

Some blogs may have a Notify Me of Follow Up Comments via Email check box. This option allows readers to be notified when responses are made to their comments. This feature allows them to follow the discussion more easily without having to return to the article periodically.

After readers complete the information and click the **Submit Comment** button, the comment is recorded.

For cases in which a reader is already logged in to WordPress (that is, they operate their own blog on WordPress.com), they are not prompted for name, email, or website and can leave the comments by filling in the comments text area and clicking the **Submit Comment** button.

> NOTE: **Finding Other Blogs**
> You can find other blogs on WordPress.com by entering text in the search box in the upper right. You can also log in to WordPress.com and click either the Freshly Pressed or Tags tab just below the WordPress.com logo.

# Allowing or Denying Comments

You decide whether you want to allow or deny comments on an article. When you allow comments, it shows that you are open to feedback and encourages discussion. Discussions build author-to-reader and reader-to-reader relationships that build loyalty. Most sites, even some of the really big news sites, enable their readers to leave comments.

There is nothing wrong with denying the use of comments in your blog, but you must recognize that denying comments sends a much different message to your readers. Human beings are social creatures and like interaction; that is why social media sites are growing so fast. Blogging is just one form of social media. By choosing to disallow comments, your readers are likely to perceive you as closed off and aloof. This is generally a bad thing on the Internet today. Whether you receive one comment a year or 1,000 a day, WordPress makes it easy to manage your comment traffic.

# Reviewing the Discussion Settings

We covered many of the settings that control the default behavior for comments in Lesson 4, "Configuring Your Blog Settings." You can find the settings for comments on the side menu under Settings, Discussion. These settings control whether your readers can leave comments, how long comments are available for an article, how much information readers need to provide when leaving comments, and so on. You should review all these settings as you develop a comment management strategy.

The three check boxes at the top of the Discussion Settings screen (see Figure 5.3) are of particular interest because they can be overridden by settings on each article. The first two deal with interaction between WordPress blogs, and the last one is between your reader and your blog. The first three settings are as follows:

- ► **Attempt to Notify Any Blogs Linked To from the Article—** Notice this setting says "attempt." It does not ensure that you will be successful when you reference other blog addresses in your post. Your success depends on how their settings are configured.

- ► **Allow Link Notifications from Other Blogs (Pingbacks and Trackbacks)—**This setting controls whether your blog accepts pingbacks and trackbacks from other blogs. It is the other half of the equation to the first setting.

- ► **Allow People to Post Comments on New Articles—**Use this check box to establish whether you allow readers to make comments. If this setting is checked, the check box at the bottom of the New Page or New Post page is also checked. If it is unchecked, the default on those pages is off also. Depending on the theme, readers may still see a prompt to leave a comment even if this setting has been disabled.

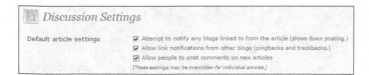

**FIGURE 5.3**   The first three Discussion Settings control the default for an individual article but can be overridden by settings on each individual page or post.

---

PLAIN ENGLISH: **Pingbacks and Trackbacks**

Pingbacks and trackbacks are electronic "tips of the hat" to let others know you mentioned them. They are a way for blogs to communicate with each other. For example, if I leave a link in one of my articles to an article in Kreg's WordPress blog and configure my blog to send notifications, he gets an email with a link to my reference as long as his blog is set up to receive these notifications. It's not a bad idea to know what people are saying about you. It is best practice to leave these incoming notices turned on.

There are differences between trackbacks and pingbacks. For more information, visit http://codex.wordpress.org/Introduction_to_Blogging and review "Managing Comments" within the "Things Bloggers Need to Know" section.

---

# Changing the Setting for Individual Articles

As you create or edit an article, look near the bottom of the screen for a section labeled Discussion (see Figure 5.4). You might have to scroll to find it. If you do not see it, check your Screen Options to ensure it has not been turned off.

**FIGURE 5.4**   The Discussion Settings on an individual article override the global Discussion Settings.

The first setting allows or disallows readers to leave comments. Just because someone can leave a comment does not mean the comment is automatically displayed to the public. Refer to "Managing Comments" in this lesson for more information.

The second setting allows or disallows other blogs to notify you of a reference to your article. These blogs may still create a link from their site to yours, but you won't be notified if this setting is not turned on.

# Dealing with Comment Spam

All this communication between people and blogs sounds wonderful. It is easy for people to leave comments, and because the process is so easy and open, some people try to exploit it by sending you unwanted comments known as spam. For the first couple of years of WordPress's life, spam was not a major issue. As WordPress grew, so did the target.

To be fair, you are not likely to get too many comments (good or bad) when you first get set up. Unless you are a national TV or radio personality, or you are in a band with 100,000 fans, your site will not be of much interest to comment spammers right away. Comment spammers often target high-profile sites or sites that have been around for some time. When you are just starting out, the spammers won't know you exist. As your blog is linked to, and mentioned by, others, your profile will grow.

Typically, comment spammers find an old post, perhaps a year or two old and start adding their unwanted comments there. One way to limit this practice is to turn off the ability for readers to make comments after a certain amount of time. Refer to the section about Discussion Settings in Lesson 4 or more information on this feature.

WordPress deals with comment spam with a software extension (or plug-in) called Akismet. Like email spam filters, Akismet uses a complex formula of words and phrases to identify legitimate and unwanted comments. If a spam message passes through Akismet's filter, you can identify the comment as spam (see "Managing Comments" in this lesson), and Akismet will learn from its error to capture similar messages in the future. The learning process is not limited to only your input. Akismet's database of comment spam is a collection of all WordPress blogs, which increases the power of the software. This feature is enabled automatically and is not configurable if you are using WordPress.com. However, WordPress.org administrators need to configure it manually. Refer to Lesson 11, "Customizing Your Site with Plug-ins," for more information about plug-ins and Akismet. Whether you are using WordPress.com or hosting your own site using the software from WordPress.org, you can quickly see how effective Akismet is by viewing the information at the bottom of the Right Now Dashboard widget (see Figure 5.5). Akismet does not delete any comment spam in the event that it gets a false positive. Click the **Comments** link in the Akismet information to see a list of comments that Akismet suspects are spam. From this list, you can review the comments and determine whether they are valid spam or should be approved and visible to the public. See "Using the Comments List" in this lesson for more information.

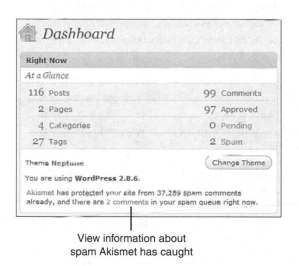

View information about
spam Akismet has caught

**FIGURE 5.5**   Akismet's stats are available from the Right Now Dashboard widget.

Don't let comment spam deter you from blogging. By using a few good practices, such as using Akismet and limiting the time an article is available for comment, you can minimize the impact of spam.

# Managing Comments

Managing comments allows you to control whether you review and approve each comment before it is made available to the public. For the new blogger, this is not a big time investment. If you allow all comments to be available to the public immediately, you could subject yourself to possible legal consequences if one of your readers makes a comment about another person or organization and the target of the comment feels he has been portrayed inaccurately. The legal ramifications of allowing and disallowing comments are beyond the scope of this book. The best way to protect yourself against being a part of a legal dispute is for you to moderate comments (using your best judgment).

You can enable comment moderation from Settings, Discussion. Check the Before a Comment appears: An Administrator Must Always Approve the Comment option. Although this option says "administrator," it refers to any person who has comment moderation capabilities for the blog. By default, this is anyone on your system with an administrator or editor role.

When you first start your blog, moderating your comments is not likely to take much time. The process is similar to the way you got started with email. You likely did not have a lot of contacts at first. You had to send mail to get mail. Your blog will grow in a similar way, and with it, the comments will grow.

If you are lucky and your blog starts to get a lot of activity, you might find yourself with a lot of incoming comments to review and approve. One option in this situation is to ask for help. Ask regular commenters if they are willing to help moderate. If you already have regular contributors, ask them if they would like to be editors to assist with comment management.

There are several ways to access comments and manage them from the Administrative Dashboard. They include

> ► The shortcut button at the top right. Using the drop-down arrow, select Comments (see Figure 5.6).

▶ The Recent Comments widget on the Administrative Dashboard.

▶ The Comments subpanel on the side menu.

**FIGURE 5.6**   Accessing comments from the shortcuts menu in the upper right.

---

TIP: **Quickly Spot Outstanding Comment Approvals**

A number listed on the comments subpanel indicates the number of comments pending approval. No number indicates all comments have been approved.

---

# The Recent Comments Dashboard Widget

One way to manage the incoming comments is to use the Recent Comments widget on the Administrative Dashboard (see Figure 5.7). If the widget is not displayed, check the Screen Options in the upper right to ensure it has not been unchecked (turned off) at some point.

**Recent Comments**

From Scott Gallatin on Children's toy inspires cheap way to produce high tech diagnostic chips #
That's so cool!
Unapprove | Reply | Edit | Spam | Trash

From Chuck Tomasi on Hey Jude – the flowchart #
We need one more arrow from the top "hey jude" to the bottom "na" for the second half of the ...

From book review on Hey Jude – the flowchart #
The beatles?

From D. Ebdrup on Wow...Check out this Eight Foot Tall Robot #
I, for one, welcome our new overlords.

From Chuck on CCT#237: ...With Kreg and Chuck – 206.222.2428 #
Happy to Help. More to come Steve

View all

**FIGURE 5.7**   The Recent Comments Dashboard widget makes it easy to quickly approve, trash, edit, reply to, or mark as spam incoming comments.

By default, this widget shows the five most recent comments to your system. New comments awaiting moderation are highlighted in yellow. As you pass your cursor over each comment, several options appear just below the text of the comment. They include

- ▶ **Approve (or Unapprove)**—If a new comment is awaiting approval, click the **Approve** link to have it show up in your blog. If the comment has already been approved, the link reads Unapprove. Clicking **Unapprove** removes the comment from your blog but does not delete it from your system.

- ▶ **Reply**—Using the **Reply** link is a convenient way to respond to comments without ever leaving the Dashboard.

- ▶ **Edit**—Use the Edit link to bring up the editor; change the name, email address, or URL; fix typos in a comment; or change the status or the date the comment was posted. Click the **Update Comment** button to apply your changes.

▶ **Spam**—If you encounter an unwanted comment and believe it to be spam, click **Spam** and it is removed immediately.

▶ **Trash**—Clicking the **Trash** link moves a comment to the comment Trash folder. Refer to the "List Basics" sidebar in Lesson 3, "Creating Posts and Pages," for more information on managing your trash.

Additionally, clicking the **View All** button takes you to the Comments List to see and manage more comments. This button performs the same action as the Comments subpanel on the side menu or choosing **Comments** from the shortcuts menu.

## Using the Comments List

The comments list gives you access to multiple comments at one time (see Figure 5.8). The function and layout are similar to that of other lists discussed in earlier lessons.

**FIGURE 5.8** The comments list displays many features to help manage comments.

Currently, three columns display for comments—Author, Comment, and In Response To. The Screen Options drop-down in the top right of the screen enables you to control the display of two of the following two columns:

▶ **Author**—This setting displays who wrote the comment, her email address, website (if entered), and the Internet address from which she entered this information. Clicking the web address brings you to that page. Clicking the email address composes an email using whatever client you have set up on your computer (Outlook, Outlook Express, Mac Mail, and so on). Clicking the IP address filters the comment list to comments made from the same IP address as the one listed.

▶ **In Response To**—This column displays the title of the article the comment is related to, the number of comments made on the same article, and a hash sign (#). Clicking the article title brings you to the editor. Clicking on the number of comments brings you to a filtered list of comments that are all related to the same article. Clicking on the hash sign brings you to the article as it is displayed to the public in your blog.

The only column that cannot be disabled is the Comment column. It displays the date the comment was submitted and the text of the comment. The date is a link to the blog article as it is displayed to the public in your blog. As you move your cursor over each row of the comment listing, several options appear just below the comment text. These options enable you to modify an individual comment quickly. The following options are displayed:

▶ **Approve (or Unapprove)**—If a new comment is awaiting approval, click the **Approve** link to have it show up in your blog. If it has already been approved, the link reads Unapprove. Clicking **Unapprove** removes the comment from your blog but does not delete it from your system.

▶ **Spam**—If you encounter an unwanted comment and believe it to be spam, click **Spam** and it is removed immediately.

▶ **Trash**—The Trash link moves a comment to the Trash folder.
Refer to the "List Basics" sidebar in Lesson 3 for more information
on managing your trash items.

▶ **Trash**—The Trash link moves a comment to the Trash folder.
Refer to the "List Basics" sidebar in Lesson 3 for more information
on managing your trash items.

▶ **Edit**—The **Edit** link brings you to the comment editor (see
Figure 5.9). The comment editor lets you update the various
fields associated with the comment including the commenter's
name, comment text, and so on. Click the **Update Comment**
button to apply your changes.

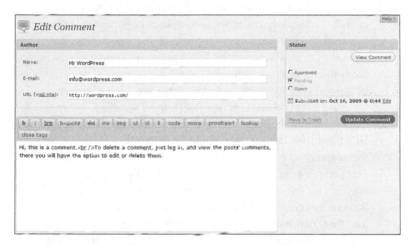

**FIGURE 5.9**   The comment editor lets you change any comment attribute.

▶ **Quick Edit**—The Quick Edit link is similar to the Edit link with
the exception that you do not go to a separate screen to make the
edits. The name, email, URL, and comment text are available to
edit directly in the list. Click the **Update Comment** button to
apply your changes or use **Cancel** to abort.

▶ **Reply**—Clicking the **Reply** link is a convenient way to respond
to comments without leaving the comment list.

Above the comment listing are several additional options to help you find comments (see Figure 5.10). They include

▶ **A search box**—The search box provides you with a simple method to find words or phrases in your comments. Simply enter the text you want to locate in the text box and click **Search Comments**. Your results are displayed in the comment listing.

▶ **All, Pending, Approved, Spam, and Trash**—The links just below the title Edit Comments provide a quick way to filter your comments based on the current status. With a single click, you can locate all comments classified as Pending (unapproved), Approved, Spam, Trash, or All (approved and unapproved) comments.

▶ **Bulk Actions**—The Bulk Actions drop-down list is used together with the check boxes on the side of each comment in the list. For example, say you want to approve all eight comments that have not yet been approved and they appear in various places in the listing (perhaps on different pages). You could locate each one, hover over the entry, and click **Approve**. That approach takes at least eight clicks and possibly some scrolling. Using a combination of the status features described in the preceding bullet and Bulk Actions, you could click **Pending** to display all the unapproved comments and then click the check box in the first column header. This approach selects all the entries displayed with one click. Finally, choose **Approve** from the Bulk Actions and click the **Apply** button. That's a total of four clicks. The Bulk Actions list also appears at the bottom of the comment listing (see Figure 5.10). The list contains the following options:

  ▶ **Unapprove**—Unapprove all selected comments. This changes the status of the selected comments to Pending and removes them from the public view.

  ▶ **Approve**—Approve all selected comments.

  ▶ **Mark as Spam**—Identify all selected comments as Spam and remove them from the system.

  ▶ **Move to Trash**—Move all selected comments to the Trash folder.

**FIGURE 5.10** Using bulk actions can save you time when managing multiple comments.

▶ **Comment Type Filter**—Displayed next to the Bulk Actions list with a default value of Show All Comment Types, this filter lets you display all types of comments, normal comments from readers, or pingbacks/trackbacks from other systems. After you select the type of comment to display, click the **Filter** button.

▶ **Check for Spam button**—This button runs all your comments through the spam filter (Akismet) again. This capability is useful if the service has learned a new spam technique and you have comments that are pending approval. This option also appears at the bottom of the comment listing.

▶ **Page index**—The page index appears on the right side just below the search box when you have more than 20 comments in your listing. You can use the page numbers to go directly to the displayed number or use the forward and backward arrows to advance one page in either direction. This option also appears at the bottom of the page listing.

## Receiving Email Notifications

It is possible to have WordPress notify you when comments are made to your blog. This capability can improve the time it takes to moderate and respond to comments because most people are in the habit of checking their email more than their blog comments. There are two options related to receiving email notifications. They are found in Settings, Discussion on the side menu. Both options use the email address found in Settings, General to send notifications. These Discussion options are found under the heading Email Me Whenever:

- ▶ **Anyone Posts a Comment**—When this option is checked, all comments generate an email notification whether they require approval or not.

- ▶ **A Comment Is Held for Moderation**—When this option is checked, an email is generated any time a comment requires approval. Note that this may not generate an email for all comments if the comment author has previously submitted comments that have been approved and the Comment Author Must Have Previously Approved Comment option is enabled.

# Best Practices

There are several guidelines for managing your comments effectively. These are by no means required rules; they are simply ideas that bloggers have found to work well.

1. Check your comments regularly. If you are using email notifications, you will be notified moments after a comment has been made (depending on the way your Discussion Settings are configured). If you are not using email notifications, make it a practice to check your comments at least twice as often as you post. If you post once a week, check for comments twice a week. If you post daily, check multiple times a day. In reality, you are likely to get comments half as often as you post, but checking more frequently gives better customer service to your readers.

2. Respond to all (nonspam) comments. Treat each comment as an invitation to a conversation. Someone has a question or feedback for you. Respond to them as you would in person. Remember that the conversation is public.

3. Use an email alias. If possible, set your General Settings email with an email alias. An email alias points to your proper address without revealing your usual address. When mail is sent to the alias, it is redirected to your mailbox. This allows you to filter incoming comment notifications and act on them based on the alias address. It also allows you to change the alias without modifying your WordPress configuration should you decide to use a distribution list or transfer responsibility of comment management to another person. Suggestions of email aliases include comments@yourdomain.com, wordpress@yourdomain.com, or feedback@yourdomain.com. Check with your mail service provider or administrator to see if you can set up an email alias for your name.

---

NOTE: **What Kinds of Comments Will I Get?**

If you write a post in which you express a strong opinion or evoke an emotional response, you should expect to get some strong comments. If you write something technically incorrect, your readers are likely to correct you. If you ask a probing question, you are likely to get answers.

---

# Summary

Comments are the primary means by which your readers and other bloggers interact with you. After you have configured your comments the way you like, management of new comments is relatively easy with the exception of an occasional spam comment.

# LESSON 6

# Personalizing the Appearance of Your Blog

*In this lesson, you learn how to give your site a whole new look and feel without a lot of work or technical skill.*

## Themes

Themes are what give a WordPress blog its personality. WordPress provides the theme functionality to allow you to easily change the look of your site without being a professional web developer. You have probably seen dozens of WordPress blogs and not realized it (including msnbc.com) because many of the blogs use a different theme than the default that's supplied with every WordPress blog (see Figure 6.1). A theme is a set of files that define font sizes, margins, screen layout, and more. Your postings, pages, links, and other settings remain the same, but the way they are presented changes. Some refer to this as "skinning" your site, but WordPress refers to it as themes.

**FIGURE 6.1**    While functional, the default theme "Kubrick" is a bit plain.

You can change a few things, such as your blog title and tagline, without getting involved with themes, but they have minimal impact on the overall personality of your site.

Themes are very easy to set up and at the same time allow you to customize nearly every aspect of WordPress. This is one area where WordPress.com and WordPress.org differ. Although the basic functionality is the same, the features vary. With WordPress.com, you can choose from dozens of themes. WordPress.org has thousands to choose from. WordPress.com allows you to do custom CSS (cascading stylesheets) with an optional upgrade fee. WordPress.org allows you to customize your CSS for no additional charge. Refer to Lesson 10, "Using Themes on Your Own Site," for more information on customizing themes on your own blog.

# Branding

Your blog reflects part of who you are, or rather whom you would like to represent online. For the sake of this lesson, I assume you are setting up a blog for your own purposes. With that assumption, selecting a theme is purely a matter of personal choice.

If you are setting up a blog for an organization or website that already has a defined brand (color scheme, logo, and so on), you should consider hosting your own blog and enlisting the help of a web developer or read one of many books on the PHP programming or cascading style sheets (CSS) to fine-tune your blog. PHP programming and CSS are beyond the scope of this book.

# Finding and Applying a New Theme

To start locating and applying a new theme, log in and click on **Appearance** on the side menu. The Manage Themes page appears, as shown in Figure 6.2.

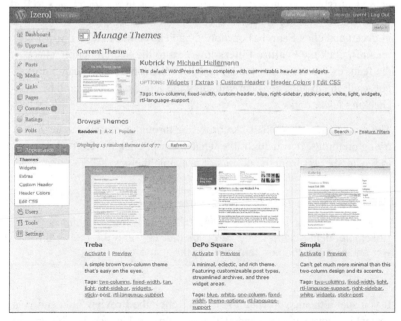

**FIGURE 6.2**  The Manage Themes page is your key to refacing your blog.

Your current theme is listed at the top of the page. There are several options available to your theme. They are covered in the "Making Additional Changes" section later in this lesson. Further down the page are 15 random themes. There are currently more than 70 different themes you can choose from. Each theme includes a thumbnail image so you get an idea of what it looks like.

NOTE: **Limited Theme Choices**

With WordPress.com, it is not possible to use themes other than the standard themes provided. However, additional themes are available to you if you host your own blog using the software available from WordPress.org. Additional information is available in Lesson 11.

Using the theme browser just under your current theme, you can find themes alphabetically, see the most popular themes, or search for a theme based on keywords (tags) or features. Each theme has one or more tags to help identify and organize it. Use these keywords in the search box to find specific attributes. For example, if you are looking for a green theme, type in **green** and click **Search**. For more complex searches based on specific features, click the **Feature Filters** link next to the Search button, check the features you are interested in, and click **Search**. If your search does not result in any hits, consider widening the scope of your search by checking fewer options.

The random search is rather like browsing through a clothing store and trying on things. If you don't like what you see, click the **Refresh** button to see another set from the dozens of available themes.

TIP: **Use Theme Tags to Find Similar Themes**

The tags for each theme are links. If you see a feature you like (for example, right sidebar), you can click that tag, and the theme browser shows more themes that contain the same tag.

If you spot a theme you want to "try on," click the **Preview** link, and your content is displayed in the window that pops up (see Figure 6.3). This preview has no impact on what the current visitors to your blog are seeing.

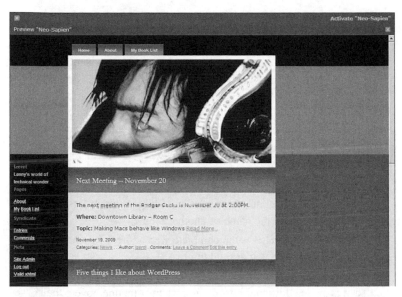

**FIGURE 6.3** The Preview link lets you see what your content looks like if you apply the theme.

If you like the theme and want to apply it to your site, click **Activate "name"** in the upper right of the preview window. If you want to keep shopping, click **X** in the upper left to close the window. Your theme represents you, so have some fun with it.

CAUTION: **Don't Change Too Often**

You can change your theme any time you like by going to the **Appearance** menu option, locating a new theme, and applying it. However, you should realize your readers may get confused if you change your theme frequently. Changing your theme changes the location of links and icons. Try to settle on a theme and make only minor changes afterward.

## Links

Links allow you to create a collection of other websites you want to share. By placing websites in your link library, you can easily present them on your front page with the Links widget. Refer to Lesson 7 for more information on

Widgets. You do not need any knowledge of HTML to display links. All you need is a title and the URL of the other site. In turn, you can request others add your blog to their links.

## Adding a New Link

To create a new link, click the **Add New** subpanel under Links on the side menu. Clicking this option displays several fields to identify your new link (see Figure 5.9). At a minimum, fill in the first two fields. Following are the link-related fields:

- ▶ **Name**—This is the name as it is displayed on your web page. It should be an accurate representation of what you are linking to—for example, the name of another blog.

- ▶ **Web Address**—This is the complete web address (including http://) of the site you are linking to.

- ▶ **Description (optional)**—You can add a description here so you can provide additional information when someone hovers their mouse cursor over the link.

- ▶ **Category (optional)**—From this field, you can select a category (or create an additional category) to organize your links.

- ▶ **Target (optional)**—If you choose, you can identify how the link is displayed with one of the following targets:

  - ▶ **_blank** causes a new browser window to appear with the linked page when the link is clicked.

  - ▶ **_top** presents the new linked page in the top frame of the current page. If your site is designed with frames, selecting this option removes existing frames.

  - ▶ **_none** is the default behavior if you choose no target; it places the content in the current window.

  This is purely a personal preference if you want new content to go in a new browser window (allowing readers to still maintain a page with your content), minimize the number of open windows (or tabs) readers have, or let them choose how they want their browser to behave.

- ▶ **Link Relationship (optional)**—The link relationship is based on a protocol called XFN, which stands for XHTML Friends Network. It allows you to identify the type of relationship you have with the people or sites you are linking to. To learn more about XFN, visit http://gmpg.org/xfn. The different types of link relationships are as follows:

- **Identity**—This check box identifies the link as one of your websites.
- **Friendship**—Select the option that most accurately represents your association with the other person or site.
- **Physical**—If you have physically met the other person (or people) face-to-face, check the Physical check box.
- **Professional**—Check this check box if the other person is a professional acquaintance (coworker or colleague).
- **Geographical**—This option identifies your geographic location in relation to the other person. Co-resident signifies you live with the other person. Neighbor is in a similar geographic region (city, town, or village). None indicates you either don't know or don't care.
- **Family**—If the other person is related to you, choose the option that best represents your relationship in the Family section.
- **Romantic**—You also have the option to select one or more options if you are romantically involved with the other person.
- **Advanced (optional)**—The Advanced section allows you to set additional options. The image address lets you link to another site's image and display it along with the link. There are two things you need to know to use this feature. First, know whether your current theme supports images in the links. Second, know the direct URL to the image you are going to use (for example, http://mydomain.com/images/logo.jpg). The RSS address allows you to specify the RSS feed alongside the site's link. Again, not all themes support this feature. Notes is a place for you to capture any additional thoughts you have about the link you have collected. There may come a point in the future when you don't recall adding the information, and these notes may be your only clue where it came from and why it was added. Finally, rating allows you to rate your links from 0 (worst) to 10 (best). Some themes sort the links by ranking.
- **Keep this link private**—This check box on the right keeps the public from viewing the link. Only site administrators can see private links.

Be sure to click **Add Link** to save your settings.

# Widgets

A widget is a tool or content that displays some type of information on the sidebars of your blog. Although themes give you control of how things are displayed on your blog, widgets enable you to control what is displayed.

Widgets make it easy to add, move, or remove content from the left or right sidebars of your blog provided you are using a widget-ready theme.

> TIP: **Use Widget-Ready Themes**
>
> When selecting a theme, look for themes that are widget ready (use the tag "widgets"). Customizations to non-widget-ready themes require HTML, CSS, and PHP programming knowledge.

You can find the Widgets page in the Appearance menu under the subpanel labeled Widgets (see Figure 6.4) or from the Widgets option on the Manage Themes page.

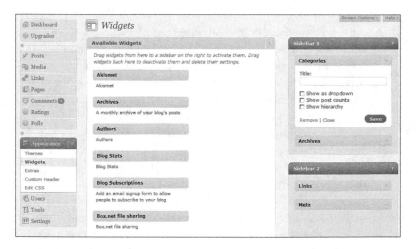

**FIGURE 6.4**   The Widgets page.

Each widget has a unique function. There are dozens of widgets and new ones being developed all the time. A few of the commonly used widgets you may want to familiarize yourself with are as follows:

▶ **Archives**—The archives widget shows a historical collection of your blog posts listed by month. After you have been blogging for a year or two, you might consider the Display as Drop Down option to save space in your sidebar.

▶ **Calendar**—The calendar widget displays a monthly calendar of your post activity with clickable links displaying all posts for that date. It does not let you set up a calendar of events. It is used only to display your post activity.

▶ **Categories**—The categories widget alphabetically lists the categories of your blogs, which makes it easier for your readers to find your content.

▶ **Links**—The links widget displays the entries you have made from the Links subpanel. The links widget is a good way to recommend other sites to your readers.

▶ **Meta**—The meta widget contains links to log in and log out, site admin, RSS feeds, and WordPress.com. If you have multiple contributors to your blog, adding the meta widget provides them with an easy way to log in.

> CAUTION: **Where's the Login Link?**
>
> If you do not use the Meta widget anywhere, no Login link is presented to administer your blog. Adding /wp-admin to the end of your blog address accomplishes the same thing—for example, http://mysite.wordpress.com/wp-admin.

▶ **Pages**—The pages widget adds a list of your blog's pages to your sidebar. This widget might not be necessary if your theme includes a navigation bar.

▶ **Search**—The search widget provides a way for readers to do a simple text search of your content. Despite all the tags and categories, some readers find it easier to search for content.

▶ **Text**—The text widget allows you to add arbitrary text or HTML to your sidebar. You can have multiple text widgets with different content in each.

More details about widgets are available at http://en.support.wordpress.com/topic/widgets-sidebars/.

# Adding Widgets

The Widgets page displays two major sections in the center and a number of sidebar boxes on the right, which vary according to your theme. The Active Widgets are available for your use. To add a widget to your blog, drag one from the Active Widget section to the appropriate sidebar section on the right. If the sidebar shows only a dark gray title bar, use the triangle to open it. This feature allows you to place widgets in that box.

If you do not place anything in a sidebar box, the theme uses whatever widgets are defined in the theme.

Most widgets have options associated with them, such as allowing you to change the title or display lists as drop-down lists. When you drag a widget to the sidebar, a triangle appears on the right of the widget title bar. Click the triangle to view and set the options. Click **Save** when you are done making changes to your widget options.

There is no Save or Update button on the Widget page. When you are done configuring the widgets, you can immediately see their effect by viewing your site.

# Removing Widgets

To remove a widget from your sidebar, drag it to either the Active Widgets or Inactive Widgets section of the screen. Both sections have the same effect in terms of removing the widget. However, if you've made any changes to the widget, such as URLs or other text, those changes are lost if you put it in Active Widgets, whereas your changes are preserved when you put the widget in Inactive Widgets.

# Making Additional Changes

In addition to using themes and widgets, there are some additional ways you can customize your blog's look and feel.

## Extras

The Extras page (see Figure 6.5) is available from Appearance, Extras or the Extras option from the Manage Themes page.

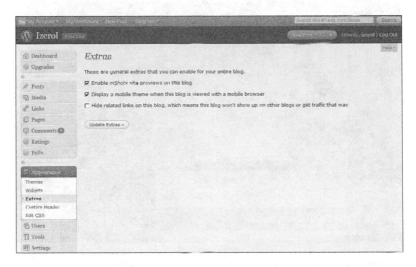

**FIGURE 6.5**   The options on the Extras page.

The Extras page has three options available that you can enable for your entire blog.

### mShots—Preview Links

mShots allows a blog reader to get a preview of the sites you link to without leaving your site. To turn on this feature, check the **Enable mShots Site Previews on This Blog** option on the Extras page. When the reader moves his mouse over a link to another site, a window pops up with a preview of that site (see Figure 6.6). The preview for some sites appears instantaneously, but some sites take a few seconds to generate a preview.

> **NOTE: Disabling mShots**
>
> Your readers can disable mShots for all WordPress.com sites by clicking **Turn Site Previews Off** in the bottom-right corner of the preview window. However, re-enabling mShots is a bit trickier. To re-enable mShots, your readers need to remove the cookie "nopreview" for the domain ".wordpress.com." Consult your browser's documentation for detailed information on managing cookies.

**FIGURE 6.6**   mShots show a preview of sites you link to.

## Mobile Browsers

The Extras page also has an option to assist readers with mobile browsers. When you check the **Display a Mobile Theme When This Blog Is Viewed with a mobile browser** setting, you enable one of two mobile themes specially designed for readers using the browser on their mobile devices (see Figure 6.7). The themes are designed to load quickly. The first is designed specifically for the iPhone, iPod Touch, and Android phones. This theme takes advantage of some of the browsing capability of the platform, giving readers access to the following:

▶  Posts, pages, and archives

▶  Commenting and post loading using AJAX (for faster interaction)

▶  Scaled header images if a custom image is used

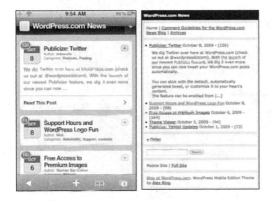

**FIGURE 6.7**    Two theme options available to mobile browsers.

When readers view your site with the mobile theme, the layout does not appear as with a desktop browser. iPhone, iPod Touch, and Android users can switch to your normal theme by turning off the mobile site option at the bottom of the page.

Other mobile browsers get a less fancy theme but still get quick load times. These browsers have a Full Site link at the bottom of the page. The effectiveness of this link is browser dependent.

## Possibly Related Posts

WordPress.com came out with a feature called "lateral navigation" that scans the content of your post and then displays other posts from other blogs that may be related (see Figure 6.8).

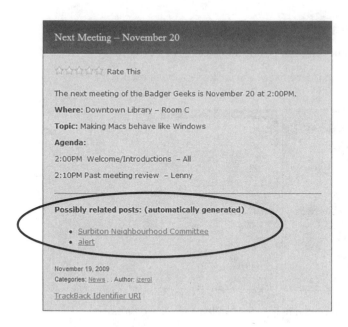

**FIGURE 6.8**   Possibly Related Posts can point your readers to similar material.

Some blog administrators find this feature annoying, stating that it takes readers away from their blog. The feature is controlled by the Hide Related Links on This Blog option in Appearance, Extras. If you remove related links from your blog, WordPress removes you from other blogs also—which can impact traffic to your site.

If you have made any changes to the Extras page, click **Update Extras** to save your changes.

## Custom Header Image

Some of the WordPress.com themes look terrific. However, you might think that the header image does not match your personal tastes. Fortunately, some of the themes, including the default (Kubrick), enable you to upload your own header image.

To find out which themes support custom headers, follow these steps:

1. Go to **Appearance, Themes**.

2. In the Browse Themes section, click the **Feature Filter** link.

3. Check the **Custom Header** option.

4. Click **Apply Filters**.

The first 15 themes that support custom headers are displayed. Activate the theme you would like to use.

To change the header image, follow these steps:

1. Go to **Appearance, Custom Header** or the **Custom Header** link at the top of the Manage Themes page to see the Header Image page (see Figure 6.9).

2. Click the **Browse** button (or **Choose File** button on a Mac) to locate an image file on your computer.

3. After you locate an image, click **Open** (or **Choose** on a Mac).

4. Click **Upload**.

5. When your image is finished uploading, it is displayed with a highlighted rectangle.

6. Drag and resize the rectangle to crop the image the way you like. The rectangle stays the same proportions to the original image to ensure it is not stretched when it is displayed at the top of your blog.

7. Click **Crop Header**.

8. View your blog front page.

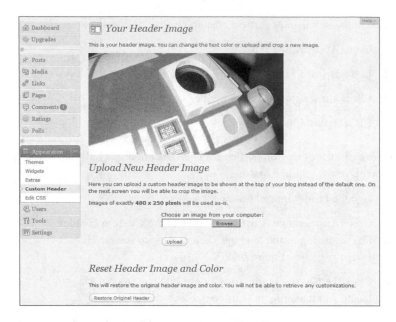

**FIGURE 6.9**    It is possible to upload a new header image with many themes.

You can restore the original header image at any time from the Header Image page by clicking the **Restore Original Header** button.

# Edit CSS

The Edit CSS option allows you to fine-tune the appearance of your site by creating your own cascading style sheet (CSS) or augmenting the current theme's CSS. To get to the CSS Stylesheet Editor page (see Figure 6.10), go to **Appearance**, **Edit CSS** in the side menu.

**FIGURE 6.10** The CSS Stylesheet Editor allows you to fine-tune your site appearance.

---

NOTE: **CSS Customizations Require Upgrade**

CSS customizations are a paid upgrade to WordPress.com users. You can modify the style sheet and preview the effect your changes have, but you cannot apply them to your site without the upgrade. Go to **Dashboard**, **Upgrades** for details and current pricing.

---

By default, a placeholder message appears in the main text box. This message is entirely comments (denoted by starting with **/\*** and ending with **\*/**). Please review these comments before proceeding.

To enter your modifications, remove the existing text and enter your CSS.

PLAIN ENGLISH: **Cascading Style Sheets**

Cascading style sheets provide a set of style templates that define colors, fonts, image sizes, backgrounds, and more. They free the software author from thinking about the layout details. CSS also enable themes to allow third parties to customize the look and feel of the software package.

Just below the editing window are two options affecting how your changes are applied to your blog's theme:

- ▶ **Add This to the (Current) Theme's CSS Stylesheet**—This option augments your changes to the theme's existing style sheet. There are specific ways to override styles that you need to be aware of. Click the **View Original Stylesheet** link to display the theme's current settings.

- ▶ **Start from Scratch and Just Use This**—Choose this option if you want to build the entire style sheet. You still need to comply with the theme's HTML structure. You can refer to the original style sheet to ensure you include all rules/styles. If you miss something, your blog may not appear as you expected.

The Limit Width option modifies the default image size for full-size images, videos, and other media when it is inserted in your blog. Use this option if you have modified the main content area using custom CSS. It does not change the width of existing images and videos, nor does it change the width of your blog.

After you complete your changes, you can see what effect the changes have by using the **Preview** button. If you have not purchased the Custom CSS upgrade, you will not be able to save your changes. Otherwise, use the **Save Stylesheet** button to apply the changes to your site.

If you find something that was once working is suddenly behaving unexpectedly, you can use the CSS Revisions section at the bottom of the Edit CSS page to review and reverse changes that you have made. Each time you click the **Save Stylesheet** button, an entry in the revision history is made.

Here are some suggestions to make your learning CSS curve a bit easier if you are just getting started:

1. **Read.** There are lots of good books and websites that can guide you through cascading style sheets. Online resources include

    ▶ W3 Schools CSS material: www.w3schools.com/css/

    ▶ Web Design Group guide to CSS: www.htmlhelp.com/reference/css

    ▶ Editing WordPress CSS: en.support.wordpress.com/editing-css

    ▶ CSS 2.1 Specification: www.w3.org/TR/CSS21

2. **Start with small changes.** Begin your changes with a simple color modification or font family change and understand what impact your changes have.

3. **Use a validation service.** Free websites like http://jigsaw.w3.org/css-validator are set up to ensure you avoid errors by checking for proper CSS syntax and semantics.

4. **Use the Firebug add-on or Web Developer Toolbar (Firefox users).** Firefox has add-ons that allow you to see and modify CSS on a live page. If you use another browser, use your browser's **View, Source** option to understand where specific styles are applied.

# Summary

Using themes and widgets, you can quickly give your blog an entirely new look and feel without in-depth web development knowledge. With the optional upgrade to customize the style sheet, you can further refine your blog's appearance. The personality of your blog is limited only by your imagination.

# LESSON 7

# Using RSS and Data Migration Tools

*In this lesson, you learn what RSS is, the value of having an RSS feed, and how to set one up. You also learn how to back up and migrate your data to another blog.*

## Syndicate Your Blog with RSS

RSS stands for Really Simple Syndication. It is a method by which readers can subscribe to your blog by means of an RSS file, often called an RSS feed.

When your readers subscribe to RSS, they don't have to visit your website periodically to check for new content. Instead, programs such as Mozilla Thunderbird, Google Reader, NetNewsWire, Microsoft Outlook, and Internet Explorer download the RSS files from all sites readers subscribe to at regular intervals. The postings are then displayed much like email to make it easy for the readers to quickly glance over the headlines and open postings that are of interest.

RSS feeds are available from most blog and news sites. They are typically indicated by an orange icon (see Figure 7.1) or the words *RSS* or *Subscribe*.

**FIGURE 7.1**   The RSS icon is a quick way to indicate people can subscribe to a site.

> TIP: **Add an RSS Feed**
>
> If your blog does not currently have an RSS feed available, consider adding one to increase readership. With RSS functionality becoming more popular in applications, a large number of people on the Internet use RSS readers almost exclusively for content delivery (see Figure 7.2).

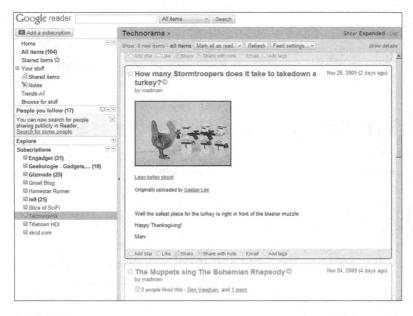

**FIGURE 7.2**    RSS applications like Google Reader deliver websites directly to you.

# Setting Up an RSS Feed

You can set up RSS feeds for posts or comments. The most common feed is the one containing your most recent posts. To create an RSS feed, follow these steps:

1. Select **Appearance**, **Widgets**.

2. Add the RSS Links widget to your sidebar by dragging it from Active (or Inactive) widgets to the sidebar.

3. Click the downward-facing triangle on the right side of the RSS widget (see Figure 7.3).

**FIGURE 7.3**   Use the RSS Links widget to allow your readers to subscribe to your blog.

4. Provide a title for your sidebar widget. Many people simply put "Subscribe".

5. Indicate which feeds to display. You can choose to have either a feed for your posts, a feed for your comments feed, or one of each.

6. Select how your feed links will be displayed with the Format option. You can choose to display an RSS icon (image), text, or both. If you choose to display an image, two additional options appear that let you set the image size (small, medium, or large) and the image color.

7. Click the **Save** button to save your changes and then **Close** to close the widget.

Now when readers want to subscribe to a feed on your site, they right-click on the orange icon, copy the link location, and paste it into their RSS reader. From then on, they will automatically know when you have posted something to your site.

Your link shows up on your page similar to the one shown in Figure 7.4.

**FIGURE 7.4**    Sample RSS links and icons using the RSS Links widget.

# Adding Other RSS Feeds

You can also add feeds to other sites using the same widget by including their RSS feed. Having a feed from another blog is useful if you have multiple blogs that are related and want to show the latest content from one on the other. For example, I have a personal blog that has a sidebar widget with links from my various podcasts. When I update one of the podcasts, the content on my personal blog is updated automatically via the RSS feed (see Figure 7.5). To obtain the RSS feed from another site, follow these steps:

1. Visit another website or blog and look for the orange icon, *Subscribe*, or *RSS*.

2. Right-click and choose the option to copy the link location.

3. Paste the link location into your RSS feed URL space in the RSS widget.

4. Click the **Save** button and then the **Close** link.

**FIGURE 7.5**    The RSS widget allows you to show content from another feed on your site.

# Using a Redirected Feed

An RSS feed is a convenience for your readers. However, you might want to better understand how many people are subscribed to your feed and what posts are generating traffic. You can do that by using a redirected feed.

Using a redirected feed might sound like something the "big guys" use to track statistics and drive traffic, but it's also useful for occasional bloggers to just find out the health of their feed.

A common way to do this is to create one feed that you make public and keep your real feed private. The public feed sends subscribers through a service that gathers statistical information about their habits. One popular service is called FeedBurner. It offers basic stats free and extended services for a fee. To get set up with FeedBurner, do the following:

1. Go to the FeedBurner site (http://feedburner.google.com).

2. Create an account or log in with your Google account if you already have one.

3. Enter your blog or RSS feed URL in the box under the label Burn a Feed Right This Instant (see Figure 7.6).

4. Click **Next**.

5. Edit the Feed Title and Feed Address if necessary. In most cases, the default values work fine.

6. Click **Next**.

7. The critical part is done. FeedBurner displays the URL of the feed you can publish to the public. Use this as the URL in your RSS widget described earlier. If you want to collect additional feed stats, click **Next** one more time and check the options you like; otherwise, click **Skip Directly to Feed Management**.

8. Click **Next**.

Log in to FeedBurner and check your stats, growth, and readers' behaviors at any time.

Enter your blog address or RSS URL

**FIGURE 7.6**   FeedBurner makes it easy to collect subscriber statistics.

> TIP: **Set Up a Redirected Feed Right Away**
>
> If you are considering gathering statistics about your blog, it is strongly recommended that you establish and publish the redirected feed right away. If you make your default WordPress feed and then decide to gather stats with a redirected feed later, all your readers will have to unsubscribe from the original feed and resubscribe to the new feed, which can cause you to lose some of your audience.

# Other Useful Tools

Several other useful tools in WordPress don't seem to fit anywhere else in the side menu, so they are placed under Tools, Tools.

## Turbo: Gears Status

Gears is a way to speed up your blog experience. Normally, your web browser has to download everything from your blog to your local computer each time you perform an operation like editing a post. Turbo mode uses a Google technology known as Gears to download certain pieces of the system to your local machine so it doesn't have to be downloaded each time—making your blog tasks faster.

> CAUTION: **Gears Support for Mac OS X**
>
> At this time, Gears is not compatible with Mac OS X higher than 10.5 (Leopard).

Gears currently supports Firefox version 1.5 and higher, Internet Explorer version 6 and higher, and Safari 3.1.1 and higher. To use Turbo mode, follow these steps:

1. From the side menu in WordPress, select **Tools, Tools**.

2. In the Turbo section, click **Install Now**.

3. If get a Gears Security Window, check the setting labeled **I Trust This Site. Allow It to Use Gears** and click **Allow**.

4. Click Install Gears from the Google site (see Figure 7.7). The download link recognizes and defaults to your current computer system (Windows, Mac, and so on).

5. Review the terms of service and click **Agree and Download**.

6. Run the installer that gets downloaded and restart your browser if instructed to do so.

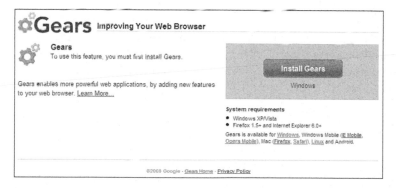

**FIGURE 7.7**   You need to download Google Gears and allow it access to use Turbo mode.

Downloading the necessary components may take a minute or two. When the process is complete, you are using Turbo mode.

> NOTE: **Results Will Vary**
>
> If you have a high-speed Internet connection, you may not see a marked improvement in performance.

# Press This

Press This is a small web application that streamlines the process of posting articles as you are browsing around the Web. As you are browsing the Internet and come across text, images, or video you want to reference, you can use Press This to quickly make a post in your blog.

You can find Press This under Tools, Tools in the side menu. To start using Press This, follow these steps:

1. Either drag the **Press This** link to your browser's link bar or add it as a favorite.

2. Find a story you like and then click the Press This link (or favorite).

3. The Press This window appears with the title and link in the article body already filled in (see Figure 7.8). Add your additional text, images, categories, tags, and other standard post material.

4. Click **Publish**.

Your post has been published. Press This offers you the options to view your post, edit your post, or close the window. When you are done, your main browser window is still where you left it. Press This can be a real time saver.

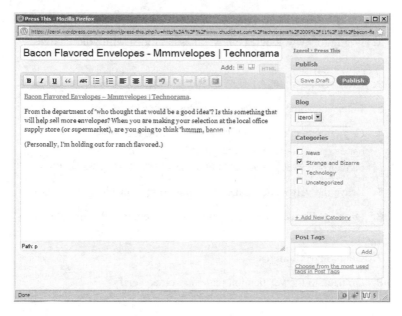

**FIGURE 7.8** Grab bits of the Internet and post it back to your blog with Press This.

# Webmaster Tools Verification

Google, Bing, and Yahoo! offer tools that provide you with detailed information and statistics about how your readers access and index your website. They can provide you with additional information to the standard WordPress statistics. Using the webmaster tools is completely optional. You can verify your site with one or all if you like with no impact to your site's performance or your readers' experience.

Before you can use these tools, you need to sign up for an account with the service of your choice and verify your blog. Use the instructions from the appropriate following section to verify your blog with one or more of the services.

## Google Webmaster Tools

1. Log in to www.google.com/webmasters/tools/ with your Google account.

2. Click **Add a site**.

3. Enter your blog URL then click **Continue**.

4. Copy the meta tag, which looks something like `<meta name='google-site-verification' content='dBw5CvburAxi537Rp9qi5uG2174Vb6JwHwIRwPSLIK8'>`.

5. Leave the verification page open and go to your blog Dashboard.

6. Open the **Tools, Tools** page and paste the code in the appropriate field.

7. Click **Save Changes**.

8. Go back to the verification page and click **Verify**.

## Yahoo! Site Explorer

1. Log in to https://siteexplorer.search.yahoo.com/ with your Yahoo! account.

2. Enter your blog URL and click **Add My Site**.

3. You are presented with several authentication methods. Choose **By Adding a META Tag to My Home Page**.

4. Copy the meta tag, which looks something like `<meta name='y_key' content='3236dee82aabe064'>`.

5. Leave the verification page open and go to your blog Dashboard.

6. Open the **Tools, Tools** page and paste the code in the appropriate field.

7. Click **Save Changes**.

8. Go back to the verification page and click **Ready to Authenticate**.

9. Go to the main page using the **My Sites** link on the left. In the status column, look for a green check mark indicating your site has been validated.

## Bing Webmaster Center

1. Log in to www.bing.com/webmaster with your Live! account.

2. Click **Add a Site**.

3. Enter your blog URL and click **Submit**.

4. Copy the meta tag from the text area at the bottom. It looks something like `<meta name='msvalidate.01' content='12C1203B5086AECE94EB3A3D9830B2E'>`.

5. Leave the verification page open and go to your blog Dashboard.

6. Open the **Tools, Tools** page and paste the code in the appropriate field.

7. Click **Save Changes**.

8. Go back to the verification page and click **Return to the Site List**.

---

NOTE: **Authentication Takes Time**

Most authentication with Google, Yahoo, or Bing happens within a few minutes; however, it might take up to 24 hours.

---

After you've got your site validated, you can use the webmaster tools to leverage the power of these search engines to determine who is linking to your site, what pages are most popular, and other statistics. You can even block the search engines from indexing part of your blog if you have pages you would like to exclude.

# Backing Up Your Data

Computers are not perfect. Sooner or later, we all lose data. To reduce your risk, make regular backups of your information including your blog data.

The way to make backups of your WordPress data is to go to **Tools**, **Export** in the side menu. Fortunately, this is one of the easiest things to do in WordPress; there is only one button! (See Figure 7.9.)

**FIGURE 7.9**    Use the export feature to back up or migrate your blog data.

When you click the **Download Export File** button, WordPress saves all your information in a file and sends it to your computer. Save the file on your computer. If you ever need to restore the information, you can use the Import feature.

> **NOTE: Take Note Where You Save Your Export File**
>
> Mac OS X automatically saves the file in your Download folder, whereas Windows users need to tell the computer to open or save the file. Be sure you know where your browser is saving the file in the event you ever need to import it.

# Migrating Your Blog

There are several reasons why you might want to move your blog data from one WordPress instance to another. You may be starting your own website with its own hosted WordPress blog, or you want to change the name of your blog and keep the content, or you want to transfer owner-ship and control of the blog to another user account. WordPress has a way to address all these requirements.

If you are starting your own hosted website, the process is as follows:

1. Register your domain.

2. Download the software from WordPress.org.

3. Install the WordPress software.

4. Export the data from your current blog (refer to "Backing Up Your Data" earlier in this lesson).

5. Import the data to your new blog (refer to "Importing Data from a WordPress Export" in the next section).

The first three steps are covered in greater detail in Lesson 8, "Setting Up Hosting."

If you are renaming your blog or migrating from one WordPress.com blog to another, the process is similar:

1. Register the new blog (refer to Lesson 1, "Introducing WordPress").

2. Export the data from your current blog (refer to "Backing Up Your Data" earlier in this lesson).

3. Import the data to your new blog (refer to "Importing Data from a WordPress Export" in the next section).

---

NOTE: **Media Not Included**

Creating an export file only exports the posts, pages, comments, categories, and tags. With the exception of migrating between two WordPress.com sites, you need to manually migrate the media files. If you have a large number of files and are migrating from one WordPress.com blog to another, you can contact support at http://en.support.wordpress.com/contact for assistance.

# Importing Data from a WordPress Export

If you are importing from a previously exported WordPress (XML) file, follow these steps:

1. Log in to your blog as an administrator.

2. Go to **Tools**, **Import** in the side menu.

3. Choose **WordPress** from the list.

4. Select and import the file. Click the browse button and navigate to your export file. WordPress names the exported file wordpress.date.xml, where date is in the *year-month-date* format, such as wordpress.2009-11-30.xml. When you've located the file, select it and click **Open**. On the WordPress page, click the **Upload file and import** button.

5. Map the authors in the export file to users on the blog. For each author, you may choose to map to an existing user on the blog or to create a new user.

6. Check the box marked **Download and import attachments**. This downloads the media library from the original site if possible. This option is only available if you are migrating between two WordPress.com sites.

7. Click **Submit**. A screen is displayed indicating the import has started. You will receive an email when it is complete.

8. WordPress then imports each of the posts, comments, and categories contained in this file into your new blog.

The import could take up to 24 hours, depending on the amount of data in your blog. You will receive an email when the import is complete. If you do not, contact WordPress.com support at http://en.support.wordpress.com/contact. When the import is complete, review your new blog to ensure everything migrated correctly.

# Transferring a Blog

WordPress allows you to transfer your blog to another WordPress.com user. You may choose to do this to transfer ownership to someone new, or you may have created a new account for yourself and want all your previously independent blogs under one account. The procedure to transfer a blog is as follows:

1. Log in as an administrator.

2. Go to **Dashboard**, **My Blogs**.

3. Move your cursor over the address of the blog you want to transfer.

4. Click on the **Transfer Blog** link. Note that you do not see this link if you are not the owner.

5. Read and review the Big Important Warning that appears. It is important that you understand all the terms and conditions of the transfer. This procedure cannot be undone (see Figure 7.10).

6. Check the check box on the bottom of the warning.

7. Enter the WordPress.com account or email address of the person you are transferring the blog to and click the **Transfer Blog** button.

8. A confirmation email is sent to your registered WordPress email address. The transfer does not occur until you read the message and click the link in email.

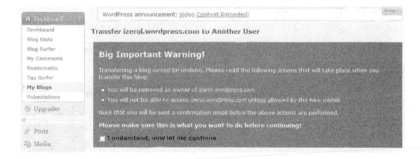

**FIGURE 7.10** Transferring a blog to another user cannot be undone.

---

NOTE: **Upgrades Transfer, Too**

Upgrades to a blog are transferred with that blog to the new owner. A blog with domain upgrades is processed manually by a member of the WordPress.com staff. All other upgrades (space, videopress, and so on) are processed automatically.

# Importing from Another Blog

If you have set up a blog on another site, WordPress allows you to import the content from that blog using the **Tools, Import** feature (see Figure 7.11). You can import from several other blogging platforms (including other WordPress sites).

Currently, it is possible to import your content from the following blogs:

▶ Blogger

▶ LiveJournal

▶ Movable Type or TypePad

▶ WordPress

▶ Yahoo! 360

Each import tool walks you through the specific steps to import your data from your old blog to your new one. Follow the onscreen instructions for your particular situation. The importer is used only to retrieve the content. It does not import any themes, images, or media files you may have had on your other blog. In some cases, the importer brings in only posts and comments (Blogger). When you import from another WordPress blog, you can restore posts, pages, comments, custom fields, categories, and tags.

In addition, you can also import links and convert WordPress tags to categories and vice versa using **Tools, Import** (WordPress.org only).

Importing from Blogger, TypePad, or LiveJournal might seem like a logical thing to do if you are just getting set up with a WordPress blog; however, the WordPress option might not seem like an obvious choice at first. There are a few reasons why you might choose this option:

▶ **Restoring a previous backup of your blog**. Some people like to have two sites. The first is a public site that they want highly available, often called a *production site*. The second is a *sandbox* (or development) site where they can make changes without the public noticing. After they have made the necessary changes in development, they can promote the changes quickly from the development site to the production site. Periodically, they might want to refresh the information in development with the more current information in production. This is done by first creating an export file (covered later in this lesson) and then using the import to update the development site.

▶ **Migrating from the WordPress.com to WordPress.org site**. You might find that WordPress.com's features are too constraining and you would like to host your own blog. Similar to the preceding scenario, you import an existing WordPress export file to bring over the content. The import subpanel is available in the self-hosted software discussed in greater detail starting in Lesson 8, "Setting Up Hosting." To learn more about how to migrate your blog from WordPress.com to WordPress.org, read the sections at the end of this lesson.

▶ **Renaming your blog**. You might find at some point that your blog name and URL do not match the brand of content you are providing. You cannot rename the WordPress.com URL, but you can register a new blog and migrate the information from your old blog to your new blog.

**FIGURE 7.11**    The Import subpanel allows you to import your blog data from another location.

# Summary

Your WordPress.com blog is set up, and you have the skills to create the content you need and make it appear in a variety of formats. Now you have the necessary information to make it easy for readers to get your posts automatically with RSS. When you are ready to move to another WordPress blog or just make a backup to ensure your work's safety, WordPress has you covered there too.

# Setting Up Hosting

*This lesson discusses why you might want to install your own copy of WordPress, including the advantages and disadvantages of doing that, and what to look for in a web hosting service. You also find out how to sign up for a domain and hosting services.*

## Why Host Your Own Blog?

WordPress is an amazing piece of software and can really shine when you do your own custom installation. There are a lot of reasons why you may or may not want to install it yourself. Perhaps you would like to install it on your company's internal network as part of an intranet solution, or you would like to use it in a custom fashion that it was not necessarily intended for, or perhaps you cannot find a web host that can offer you the options that meet your personal goals. In any case, when you are installing your own WordPress, there are certainly advantages and trade-offs to keep in mind.

One advantage that you get to exercise right out of the box is control. WordPress is licensed as open source software under the GNU General Public License (GPL). The GPL, in a nutshell, enables you to see, edit, and modify the source code as you see fit. If you have knowledge of PHP, you can have complete control of your code. If you want to make WordPress do something that it does not already do, you can. Keep in mind that learning to program is not necessary to use WordPress, and you can install WordPress without having the intention of modifying the source code.

> PLAIN ENGLISH: **Open Source and GPL**
>
> To learn more about open source software or the GPL, you can visit GPL.org at http://www.gnu.org/licenses/gpl.html. Alternatively, you can read the Wikipedia article on Open Source at http://wikipedia.org/wiki/Open_source.

When you use WordPress.com, you save money by using a free hosting service, but you are restricted in what you can to do with your site. WordPress is rich with downloadable themes and plug-ins that allow you to do pretty much whatever you want to do with your site. So hosting your own site gives you a finer degree of control over your entire site, including the ability for you to upload your own themes and plug-ins.

> TIP: **Look for Existing Themes and Plug-ins First**
>
> Before you start developing your own theme or plug-in, visit http://WordPress.org/extend/ and do a little searching. You are likely to find hundreds of themes and plug-ins already written for what you are trying to accomplish.

# Understanding Your Responsibilities

Although maintaining your own site gives you a larger degree of control, you need to consider the responsibilities. Some of them include providing support, monitoring for spam, maintaining your own backups, and keeping up with software updates. Although plug-ins that can assist in everyday maintenance are available, having your own installation means you need to take an active role in maintaining your site. Is this task overwhelming? Normally not, but it does increase the amount of effort you put into managing your site.

Common maintenance in upkeep with your site is also needed for functions ranging from keeping a look out for spam to approving comments to managing software updates. You can use plug-ins to help maintain your site automatically (which you can read about in Lesson 11, "Customizing Your Site with Plug-ins"). In addition, performing software updates is much easier today than in previous versions of WordPress. As of the last few versions of WordPress, you can upgrade plug-ins and even WordPress itself from your WordPress Dashboard with just a few clicks and no additional software. Historically updates had to be done manually by downloading them to your computer and then uploading all your updates using the File Transfer Protocol (FTP) service where your WordPress site resides.

Finally, you need to keep cost factoring in mind. WordPress.com offers free hosting, but if you go out on your own, you have to pay for hosting. Costs do vary from one hosting company to another so be sure that your hosting costs are manageable. It would be a disappointment to you and your readers if you had to take down the site because of costs.

# Setting Up Your Domain Name

Part of setting up hosting for your site is setting up your domain name. Your domain name is your calling card. It is what people will remember, bookmark, or tell others when referring to your site. Therefore, it is important that you choose a name that is unique to you and your site. Several sites can assist you in registering your domain, and several hosting companies not only register your domain, but also walk you through the entire process up to and including setting up your actual web space.

---

NOTE: **Finding a Registrar**

You may use any domain registrar you want, and there are hundreds to choose from. To help you start, the following short list includes some of the more well-known services:

Go Daddy—www.godaddy.com

NameCheap—www.namecheap.com/

Yummy Names—www.yummynames.com/

Network Solutions—www.networksolutions.com

---

When you register your domain name, the registration is set up for annual renewals. You don't actually own the domain name; you rent it. Domain names can cost anywhere from $4 to $30 for an entire year, depending on which service you are using and the domain type (.com, .us, and so on).

CAUTION: **Watch Out for Auto Renew**

Be aware that some registrars also have an Auto Renew setting that automatically drafts the renewal fee annually from your credit card.

To start your search, use your web browser to go to one of the several registrars. For each one, the process is essentially the same:

1. Pick a name that is simple and easy to remember. Again, this is the name that people will link to and tell others about when referring to you. If you are a company, choose wisely and remember you may want to register more than just the .com. You may want to get the .net and .info also to protect your brand. In addition, be prepared with backup domain names in case your first choice is already taken.

2. Start your search at one or several of the registrars (see Figure 8.1). Each one has a search box on the site where you can verify the availability of your domain name and register it. If your domain is taken already, you may be presented with alternatives, or you can try again with your second choice. Also, keep in mind that other top-level names such as .info, .us, and so on, may be available too, so try searching in different ways.

**FIGURE 8.1**   Searching for a domain using NameCheap.

3. After you find a name that you are happy with, the registrar walks you through the steps in registering your name, which includes payment and email notification after everything is complete.

---

TIP: **Look for Discounts**

Remember, some registrars offer hosting along with registering your domain. Taking advantage of this service can lower the cost in some cases when you bundle everything together and make it easier for you to manage. Also, registering your name for multiple years may also qualify you for a discount. Shopping around a little before settling on one company is worthwhile.

---

# Setting Up Your Web Hosting Account

After you have your domain name, it is time to set up your web hosting. The hosting service for your site is provided by companies referred to as web hosts. Web hosts provide you with a web server, disk space, and bandwidth, as well other services, including support.

Disk space at a web host is not unlike the hard drive in your computer. It is, in essence, the amount of space you are allowed to use when storing files for your website. Normally, the amount of space provided is, at a minimum, about 5GB. This is more than sufficient for most websites, but if you plan on hosting video and pictures, you will eventually need more space.

Also, be aware of limitations in bandwidth. Bandwidth is the amount of data transferred between your site and your visitors; it is normally tracked over a monthly period. Web hosts generally offer large amounts of bandwidth with the even lower-end packages, but if you are hosting your own video and audio files and perhaps photos, your bandwidth can dwindle quickly and become a big problem.

> TIP: **Plan for Disk Space and Bandwidth**
>
> Try to plan ahead regarding what files you will have on your server, such as pictures or other media that you will offer your visitors. Hosting companies charge for disk space and bandwidth and charge extra if you go over your allotment. Make sure you have room to operate and can expand at a reasonable price in the future.

## Requirements for Operating WordPress

Because you want to run WordPress for your site, you need to make sure that your web host provides what you need. The requirements for hosting WordPress are pretty basic when compared to most web applications. It requires PHP (version `4.3 or higher`) and MySQL (version `4.1.2` or higher) as a minimum. Most web hosting companies do support these technologies "out of the box" without your even having to ask for them. Some hosting companies give you an option of which operating system you would like your site to run on. WordPress is operating system agnostic, so any option should be fine.

Also, you should make sure you have FTP access to your site for two reasons. This access makes it easier to upload your files to the remote server and update graphics as needed and makes it much easier to keep your WordPress up to date with patches. FTP access is normally standard for hosting services, but it is something to keep in mind as you are shopping around.

# Finding Support

If you choose to maintain your own blog installation, you have several avenues for help with questions or problems you have. As with other open source software projects, WordPress offers support in the form of community, ranging from forums to web pages to online video tutorials on how to perform specific tasks to diagnoses of error codes. For most common problems, someone has likely had the same issue and has written about it.

WordPress is very well documented all over the Internet, and a good place to start looking for help is right at WordPress.org. If you or your company needs more personal support, several companies provide contract services such as help installing, troubleshooting, and even custom coding. More on finding support can be found in Lesson 13, "WordPress Support."

# Summary

This lesson examined the advantages and disadvantages of running your own self-hosted WordPress site, as well as setting up your domain name and web hosting in preparation to install your own WordPress.

# Installing WordPress

*In this lesson, you learn about scripting services that can help you install WordPress, and you walk through installing it manually.*

## Using Automated Script Services

Installing WordPress can be as automatic or as manual as you would like the process to be. Some web hosts even provide services that install WordPress, among other web applications, for you with little or no hassle.

> NOTE: **What You Need to Have**
>
> This lesson assumes that you have chosen a web hosting provider and are able to access your account via File Transfer Protocol (FTP). It is important that you have a hosting service and domain name because you will be uploading and possibly manipulating files and using the database server as part of the installation. You should make sure your web host supports PHP and MySQL.

### Using Script Services

Scripting services can make it easy to install WordPress or any number of web applications on your web hosting account and can also assist in keeping you up to date with security patches. The examples of scripting services described here are just two of many options.

> NOTE: **Use Your Preferred Scripting Service**
>
> To be clear, you may choose any scripting service you prefer. The services listed here are similar to most other services.

Go Daddy provides a service called Hosting Connection. If you have already purchased and set up a Go Daddy hosting account, or are planning to, the Hosting Connection can assist you in setting up your WordPress site.

After you set up your web hosting account with Go Daddy, visit the list of applications that Go Daddy offers and select WordPress. Go Daddy asks you to complete a form with some information needed to set up your blog, such as title, passwords, and so on. Go Daddy does the rest of the heavy lifting for you and notifies you after the process is complete. From there, you have a functioning blog.

Simple Scripts is a similar service that enables you to install any number of web applications on any web hosting account as long as you have FTP access. You can use the service for up to three installations; however, you can pay for these services and have Simple Scripts install a number of web applications in different places as well as help you keep your system up to date by automating software updates. Some web hosting companies offer Simple Scripts free with your account.

# Installing WordPress Manually

Now it's time to put together the pieces to create your own blog using WordPress.

## Downloading the Software from WordPress.org

To download WordPress, visit http://WordPress.org/download. From there, you can read the release notes and see the current version available.

---

TIP: **Finding Earlier Versions of WordPress**

If you need to install a previous version other than the current release, use the Release Archive link to find what you need.

---

To download, click the **Download WordPress** button (see Figure 9.1).

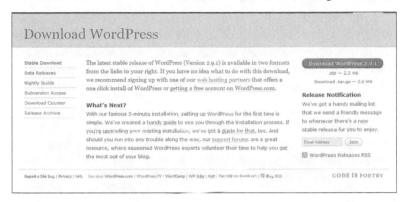

**FIGURE 9.1**   Downloading WordPress.

Your browser asks you to save the WordPress zip file to a location on your computer. Normally, this is a folder named Download, but sometimes your browser defaults to your desktop. Make a note of the location where your file is being saved so it is easy to find later.

After your download is complete, you see a new file in your download folder. Its name is similar to *WordPress-2.9.zip* (see Figure 9.2).

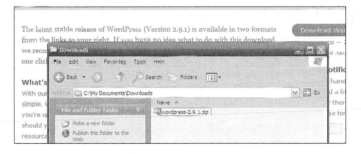

**FIGURE 9.2**   The WordPress file in the downloads folder.

# Unpacking the Software

Now that you have downloaded the WordPress zip archive from WordPress.org, we need to unpack it. A zip archive is a compressed collection of files. There are two reasons the files are compressed into a zip file. They are kept together in a container, and the file size is reduced for easy downloading. We need to open the zip archive and extract its contents.

> TIP: **Unzipping WordPress**
>
> Mac and Linux include archive software, but if you use Windows, you may not have such software installed to unzip WordPress. If you need software to unzip files, try 7-Zip at www.7-zip.org/ or WinZip at www.winzip.com/.

▶ **Mac**—Double-click on the file named WordPress-2.9.zip.

▶ **Linux**—Right-click on the WordPress-2.9.zip and select **Extract Here**.

▶ **Windows**—Right-click on the file and select **Extract Here**. After the files are extracted from the WordPress zip archive, a newly created folder named wordpress appears in your Downloads folder (see Figure 9.3). Inside the WordPress folder you just created are all the files that will make up your blog. Now it's time to upload them.

**FIGURE 9.3**    The WordPress folder after it has been unzipped.

# Uploading Your Files

After you have all your files successfully extracted out of the zip archive, you need to move them from your computer to your website. To do this, you need to plan a bit on where you are going to move them to and then you can use an FTP program to physically copy them to your webserver.

## Choosing Your Blog Folder

Before you upload your files to your web host, it is important to establish where you are going to put them. If you are adding a WordPress blog to your existing site, it is likely that you already have a main page on your site for visitors and already have a main folder created. If this is the case, you might want to put your blog in a subfolder of your website folder.

For example, you may have a Home page, photo gallery, and some other pages you have created. When you install your blog, you wouldn't want WordPress to interfere with what is already there. So it makes sense to put WordPress in a folder by itself, such as blog. Your blog site address then would be www.yoursite.com/blog.

If you are not concerned about existing content or if your site is completely new, you might want WordPress at the top level of your site so that when visitors come to your website, they are automatically greeted with your WordPress.org installation.

## Copying WordPress Files to Your Site

To upload the WordPress files to your site, you need an FTP client. An FTP client provides the functionality to log in to your remote account and upload and manipulate files. You need an FTP program to use FTP. There are many options for FTP clients, including free and pay applications. For this example, I used FileZilla. It is an open source application that costs nothing to download and use. It is available for Windows, Mac, and Linux.

---

**Note: Choosing an FTP Client**

If you want to use FileZilla, you can find it at http://filezilla-project.org/.

If you use another FTP client, you should be able to follow the steps with no trouble. FileZilla's settings are similar to other FTP clients.

Your web hosting service should have provided you with file locations, a username, and a password to access your files via FTP. Make sure you have that information handy. Follow these instructions to transfer your WordPress files via FTP to your web host:

1. Start FileZilla.

2. Click **File** and select **Site Manager**.

3. In the window that opens, click on the **New Site** button and add the name of your website on the left side of the window (see Figure 9.4).

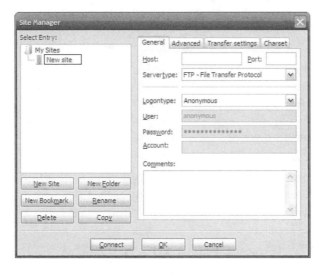

**FIGURE 9.4**    Creating a new site to transfer files to.

4. On the right side, enter the information provided by your host in the appropriate boxes. In the Host box—type the name of the server that you will be logging in to—for example, **ftp.yoursite.com**. You can leave the Port box empty.

5. Leave FTP as the selection in the Servertype box unless you have another specification from your web host.

6. Further down in the window is the Logontype box. You need to change this setting to **Ask for a Password** or **Normal**.

> CAUTION: **Always Ask for a Password**
>
> Using the Normal type allows you to specify your username and password one time. Thereafter, you are automatically logged in. In the interest of security, though, I recommend you use the Ask for a Password setting so that a password is required each time you connect.

7. After you add the necessary information, you can click on **OK** or **Connect**. Connect does just that: It saves the settings and connects you right away.

8. Now on the left side, you can view the local files that are on your computer's hard drive, and the remote files on your website are on the right side (see Figure 9.5). Not seeing any files in the remote view could be completely normal if this is a new site.

**FIGURE 9.5** Viewing local and remote files in your FTP client.

At this point, you are ready to copy over your WordPress files. On the left side of the window, navigate to the WordPress folder you created when you extracted your files from the WordPress zip file (more than likely, this folder is in your download folder). On the right side of the window, you may see a folder named public_html, htdocs, or httpdocs. This is normal. Some hosts, depending on their setup, may have a folder intended for you to put any files that you want to make public to the world, such as your WordPress files. This folder, if it exists, is called your web root folder. This is the place where you put your WordPress files. Not seeing a web root folder also could be normal, so you can just upload your files as they are.

> NOTE: **Creating a Folder for Your Blog**
>
> If you already have a site, or want to put your blog in a folder as mentioned earlier in this lesson, now is the time to create that folder on your remote site. For example, if you want to create a folder called blog, you need to create a blog folder in your web root folder. After you create a folder, double-click it to open it and then proceed to copy files into it.

In your WordPress folder, you should see several files and folders that have "wp_" at the beginning of the filename. Select all of them using the keyboard shortcut Cmd-A on a Mac or Ctrl+A on Windows. When you have them all highlighted, drag and drop them to the right side. At this point, the file transfer starts, and you see activity as the files start to upload.

After this process is complete, your local files on the left should look the same as your remote files on the right side. If they do, congratulations! You have successfully uploaded your copy of WordPress. You are now ready to create the database for WordPress to use.

# Creating the Database

WordPress needs a database to store all the posts, comments, and settings for your site. WordPress uses a MySQL database.

To create the database for your web site, you need to use the administration site provided by your web host. There are a lot of different ways your web host can give you access to your database server. No matter which administrative tool your web host uses, the basic steps to create your database for WordPress are the same.

> NOTE: **Required Database Information for WordPress**
>
> When you are done creating your database, you should have a server address, database name, username, and password. You need all that information for the last part of the installation.

1. Log in to your site's management console using the access information provided by your web host.

2. Find the section that says MySQL Server, Database Server, or something similar. Click the link to open it.

3. In the Create Database or New Database field, provide a database name. I recommend that you call your database something that is easy to recognize. For example, if your site domain name is izerol.com, consider using the database name izerol or wp_izerol.

4. You may be asked to create a username and password associated with your database. If so, be sure to make a note of this information. You will need it when running the WordPress install script. Also, make a strong password that includes numbers, uppercase and lowercase characters, and symbols. This is a place where security really matters.

It might take a little while for your database to be created after you complete these steps.

# Running the Install Script

If you have come this far, you are doing great. The installation is all downhill from here, but you are not done yet.

To finish the install, you need to run the install script. If you have uploaded all your files and created the database, you have all the tools you need to follow these steps and finish:

1. To run the installer, point your web browser to your blog's URL. You should see the first startup screen (see Figure 9.6).

There doesn't seem to be a wp-config.php file. I need this before we can get started. Need more help? We got it. You can create a wp-config.php file through a web interface, but this doesn't work for all server setups. The safest way is to manually create the file.

Create a Configuration File

**FIGURE 9.6**    Creating your wp-config file.

**2.**  Click **Create a Configuration File**.

**3.**  Gather the following information before proceeding:

  ▶ Database name

  ▶ Database username

  ▶ Database password

  ▶ Database host (the address of the server). Sometimes this can be localhost or an actual name of a server. If you are unsure, check with your web host, who should be able to provide you with that information

  ▶ Table prefix. This is a prefix for the tables in your database. If you want to run more than one WordPress installation with the same database, you can change the prefix. Doing so is not necessary for this lesson, however. On the next page, you see the prefix defaults to "wp_." Use the default.

**4.**  Click **Let's Go**. Again, the resulting screen should look familiar. Fill out these fields with the appropriate information (see Figure 9.7).

**FIGURE 9.7**    Entering your database credentials. After you have filled out these fields, click **Submit**.

Now WordPress has all the information it needs to proceed. It is ready to create your configuration file and create all the data needed for WordPress to run in the database.

5.  Click **Run the install**. If everything works as expected, the next screen asks you for some more information:

    ▶ **Blog title**—Give your blog a title. It could be a phrase, something like your business name, or "My Awesome Blog" for something personal. Feel free to be more creative than that.

    ▶ **Your E-mail**—Your email address is required in case you need to reset your Admin account password within this install of WordPress or for notifications when there are comments or other events on the blog that you need to be made aware of.

▶ Also displayed is a check box asking whether you would like your blog to appear in search engines such as Google and Technorati. Leave the box checked if you would like your blog to be visible to everyone, including search engines. Uncheck the box if you want to block search engines but allow normal visitors. For example, if you make a post about my hometown, Middling Fair, PA, when people search for "Middling Fair, PA," they will more than likely have the chance to find your post. I recommend you leave this box checked, unless you are creating a private blog.

---

NOTE: **You Can Edit Your Information**
You can change all this information after you've completed your installation by using the Administration panels.

---

6. Click **Install WordPress**, and you are taken to the final screen with your administrator username and password. The username is admin and the password is a mix of characters, numbers, and symbols. Be sure to write down this information. You need it in a moment after you click **Log In**.

At the login prompt, put in your username and the password for your admin user; then you are taken to the Dashboard for your new blog.

One final step in the completion of your installation appears at the top of your Dashboard: You are alerted that you need to change the password for the user named admin (see Figure 9.8).

**FIGURE 9.8**  Warning to change the Admin user password.

I recommend taking this opportunity to change the Admin password right away. The password provided for you is a random set of characters, but you may want to change this to something more meaningful to yourself. I also recommend making your password for Admin something good and secure, including numbers, uppercase and lowercase characters, and a symbol or two.

# Summary

In this lesson, you successfully installed WordPress. You uploaded your files, created a database on the database server, and proceeded through the install script to create a functioning blog.

# LESSON 10

# Using Themes on Your Own Site

*This lesson covers how themes can affect the form and function of your own self-hosted WordPress site and what types of layouts are available. You also will install a new theme to your newly installed blog.*

## Changing the Look and Function of Your Site

WordPress was originally intended to be a blogging platform, and it is really good for that purpose. However, you might want to use WordPress for other purposes, too. Are you are a photographer who wants to showcase your images or a cartoonist who wants to start a web comic? These are just two examples illustrating where the standard WordPress design may not suit your needs.

If you are a photographer who wants to show your work as a photo-blog, for example, you might want to display a large photograph on the front page for more of a gallery feel. Then you can include thumbnails on the side for easier navigation so that your readers can find your other works.

In the case of a web comic, you might want to show your latest comic strip at the top of the site until you post the next one and allow the readers to flip through older strips as they view your archive. And, of course, you want to keep a regular blog all at the same time.

Because there are so many WordPress themes in a variety of styles, having a clear idea of what direction you want to go can help you in your decision.

# Theme Types

When you start to look at themes, you will notice that there are as many variations of styles as there are themes for WordPress. There are fixed width, variable width, two-column, three-column, free, and premium. Before deciding on a style, first consider your blog content and readers.

If your blog is for a business, you may want something more corporate or business-like. If your blog is for you or someone else's personal site, you may not need to be so straightforward with your theme and therefore can select something more along the lines of your personality.

Finding a unique style for your blog and its voice can be a challenge. It might make sense to hire a web developer and let her design a theme from the ground up, but this task may be as simple as finding the right theme and doing a little customization. Perhaps you or someone in your organization is familiar with cascading stylesheets (CSS) and a little HTML. In that case, you can easily take a theme you find online and change it to meet your needs. Or developing your theme may be as simple as changing a logo and colors.

## Free Versus Premium

I don't want to start a debate on why premium themes are better than free themes or vice versa. I will, however, break down this issue to the lowest common denominator: You get what you pay for. There are a lot of high-quality free themes available for WordPress, many of which are available directly from the WordPress Dashboard. On the other hand, there also are a lot of high-quality premium themes for WordPress that you might like and can find simply by doing a little Internet searching.

So what do you get if you go with premium versus free?

Often premium themes come with some level of support in the form of a developer that you can contact with installation problems or even customization help. Perhaps for the cost of your theme or a few dollars more, you can have an exclusive license to use the premium theme and no one else can. This would ensure your unique look.

Alternatively, using free themes means that you can afford to change your look from time to time. You would be on your own to install or customize them, but you do get a little more freedom in return at little or no cost.

Usually, the author asks only that you include a link to his site, which is common courtesy.

Choosing between free and premium themes boils down to what your personal preferences and needs are.

## Layouts

Depending on the type of site you are running, you may need room in a sidebar for links and other functionality. Maybe you need more than one sidebar, and that is where columns come in. The number of columns you see when searching for themes refers to the structure and layout of your page.

The default theme that comes with WordPress is a two-column theme in which one column is larger than the other (see Figure 10.1). The larger column is meant to display your blog posts, and the smaller, more narrow sidebar column is meant to display links, search functions, and other widgets that you choose to display. (You can read more about widgets later in this lesson.)

**FIGURE 10.1**    The default two-column theme.

As you can see, two-column themes offer a lot of flexibility and space. They also don't take up all the browser real estate to allow for readers who have lower screen resolutions and smaller browser windows. Other options for two-column designs include having the narrow column appear on the left or right of the larger content column.

---

CAUTION: **Be Careful with Resolution**

Browser real estate is the area you can view from left to right and top to bottom when you open a web page. Some people, believe it or not, do run their computers at lower resolutions for a number of reasons, which causes the viewable area to be smaller. So if you run a theme that takes up a lot of space, it could mean that a reader may have to scroll side to side and up and down to view your site. It is common for websites to be designed with a width of between 800 and 1,000 pixels.

---

Three-column layouts are similar to two-column layouts except that they have one larger content column with two smaller columns for links. Three-column layouts are also good when you're trying to organize data that you do not want pushed below the fold of the site.

---

PLAIN ENGLISH: **The Fold**

The fold of the site refers to the bottom of your web browser that the users can't see unless they scroll down. Many websites are designed so the main content of the sites is above the fold. That way, users see the important content without having to scroll.

---

When you use the three-column layouts, it is common to place your two narrow columns either both on the left or right, or split with the content column between them. Some themes give you the option to specify how the columns are arranged, whereas others do not, so you get what you get.

## Fluid Versus Fixed Layouts

With all types of layouts, you have to decide if there is going to be extra space on either side of the content area or if your site will fill the full width of the screen. How much space the site fills is determined by fluid or fixed themes.

Using themes with fluid styles means that as you resize your browser, your site expands and contracts to fill up the space. Additionally, as visitors come to your site, they are presented with your site that fits their browser. With a fluid design, your site does not look odd with a small, fixed-width column or a compact content area if the viewer has room to display.

Fixed themes are the most predictable. Unlike fluid themes, fixed designs are essentially the same size design on anyone's browser, which offers you the advantage of having your graphics and text in a predictable format. This format is especially important if you have a theme that is image based, meaning the background and other parts of the site are made up of a series of images that need to line up correctly to look right.

# Searching for and Installing a Theme

Now that you have an understanding of the options that are available when beginning your search, you can start sorting through the large assortment of themes, choose one, and install it.

## Locating Themes

Finding a theme is probably the hardest part of installing a theme for your site. As mentioned earlier, hundreds and thousands of themes are available to you, free or otherwise, and they come in just about every color in the spectrum.

The main source for finding a theme you like is the Internet itself, and another is the WordPress.org site. Free themes are the easiest to download and try on your site, but the directions for installing a theme are the same whether the theme is free or premium.

CAUTION: **Don't Download from Just Anywhere**

Be careful downloading themes from just anywhere. The WordPress Themes directory is probably the safest place to find themes. There are reports of malicious WordPress themes that can hide links to known spam sites and run malicious code, compromising the security of your site.

## Browsing Themes at WordPress.org

You can access the WordPress database of free themes in two ways. You can access the site by pointing your browser to http://wordpress.org/extend/themes/ or you can use your WordPress Dashboard to search for and download themes directly into WordPress itself.

When you open http://wordpress.org/extend/themes/ in your web browser, you are presented with several site features that help you start looking for themes (see Figure 10.2):

▶ **Search Box**—You can search for tags or keywords that you think describe what you are looking for, such as *green* and *two-column*.

▶ **Featured Themes**—These themes are chosen randomly and change periodically.

▶ **Most Popular**—This list includes themes that get a lot of down-loads and are used by a lot of users of the WordPress Themes directory.

▶ **Newest Themes**—These themes have recently been added to the Themes directory.

▶ **Recently Updated**—These themes have been recently updated by the author.

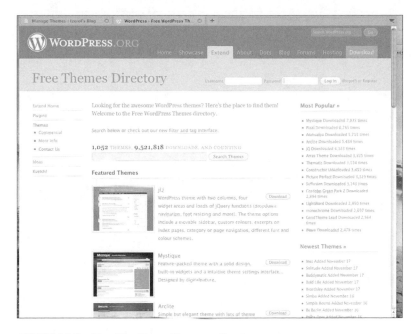

**FIGURE 10.2**   The WordPress Themes directory.

The WordPress Themes Directory is a good start and gives you several options to start browsing themes right away. All themes on the site are tagged with keywords that make them easy to search for. For example, if you search for *Photo* or *Picture*, you find WordPress themes that mostly relate to photography themes or galleries. Themes are also tagged with keywords about their layout and main color scheme.

If you are looking for a fixed-width theme that is mostly green, search for *fixed* and *green* and you see a selection of mostly fixed-width, green themes.

Additionally, when you click **Check Out Our New Filter and Tag Interface** on the main page at WordPress.org's Themes page, you are presented with a set of check boxes where you can click the keywords that you are looking for and continue your search (see Figure 10.3).

**Free Themes Directory**

Username [        ]  Password [        ]  ( Log in )

Extend Home

Plugins

Themes
- Commercial
- More Info
- Contact Us

Ideas

Kvetch!

**Tag Filter**

( Find Themes )

| Colors | Columns | Width | Features | Subject |
|---|---|---|---|---|
| ☐ black | ☐ one-column | ☐ fixed-width | ☐ custom-colors | ☐ holiday |
| ☐ blue | ☐ two-columns | ☐ flexible-width | ☐ custom-header | ☐ photoblogging |
| ☐ brown | ☐ three-columns | | ☐ theme-options | ☐ seasonal |
| ☐ green | ☐ four-columns | | ☐ threaded-comments | |
| ☐ orange | ☐ left-sidebar | | ☐ sticky-post | |
| ☐ pink | ☐ right-sidebar | | ☐ microformats | |
| ☐ purple | | | ☐ rtl-language-support | |
| ☐ red | | | ☐ translation-ready | |
| ☐ silver | | | ☐ front-page-post-form | |
| ☐ tan | | | ☐ buddypress | |
| ☐ white | | | | |
| ☐ yellow | | | | |
| ☐ dark | | | | |
| ☐ light | | | | |

**FIGURE 10.3**    Searching for themes with tag selection.

After you click on a theme and view its profile, you can see the theme's description and a link to its stats (see Figure 10.4). The stats provide you with some information on how many times it has been downloaded over time. This information might or might not be of interest to you. You might want a popular theme, which would be one that is downloaded a lot. However, you might prefer to have a unique theme, in which case you can steer clear of themes that are downloaded frequently and choose something else instead.

The description tells you a bit about this theme, providing the layout along with a thumbnail image. If you click the thumbnail or the green Preview button to the right of the page, you are presented with a large preview of the theme in action to see whether it is what you're looking for. This feature makes it much easier to shop around for a look you like.

Instead of using the WordPress site, you can also browse the same themes from inside your WordPress Dashboard (see Figure 10.5). Go to your Dashboard (www.yoursite.com/wp-admin) and log in. While you're viewing your Dashboard, on the left side there is a block that has the title Appearance. Inside the block is a link called Add New Themes. Clicking this link takes you to a search that is similar to what's on the WordPress site.

**FIGURE 10.4**   Viewing a theme's details.

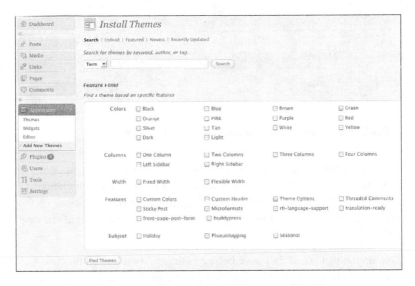

**FIGURE 10.5**   Installing themes from inside your own WordPress.

The main differences between searching for themes on the WordPress site and searching from your Dashboard are that on your Dashboard, your search results (see Figure 10.6) are displayed in a grid fashion with thumbnails and descriptions, and you have a couple of additional options.

**FIGURE 10.6**  Theme search results on your Dashboard.

Clicking **Details** gives you details on the author of the theme, ratings from other users, and the last time it was updated. Clicking on the thumbnail image or the **Preview** link brings up a larger preview, just as before on the WordPress site. To close the preview, click the **X** in the top left of the new window.

One option that you didn't have before is the ability to install themes directly from your search. To install themes directly from your search, follow these steps:

1.  Click the **Install** link, which opens the dialog box shown in Figure 10.7.

**FIGURE 10.7**    Ready to install a theme from your WordPress.

---

TIP: **Where's the Install Now Button?**

You may have to scroll down a little to see the Cancel and Install Now buttons.

---

2. Click **Install Now**.

3. Enter your File Transfer Protocol (FTP) credentials. You should have this information from an earlier lesson, or your Internet service provider (ISP) can provide that information for you.

4. Fill in this form with your username, password, hostname, and the connection type (see Figure 10.8). Usually, the Connection type is FTP unless otherwise specified by your ISP. When you are ready, click **Proceed**.

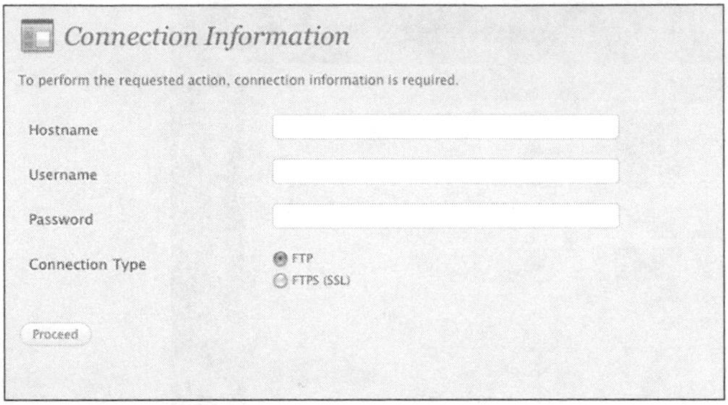

### Connection Information

To perform the requested action, connection information is required.

Hostname

Username

Password

Connection Type    ● FTP
                   ○ FTPS (SSL)

Proceed

**FIGURE 10.8**    Enter the connection information.

On the following screen, you see that your theme was downloaded, unpacked, and installed (see Figure 10.9). At this point, you can preview your theme and actually see what it looks like with information from your site. If you do preview it after installation, you also see the X at the top left to close the window, and on the right side you can activate the theme. If you click **Activate**, the theme is immediately enabled on your site.

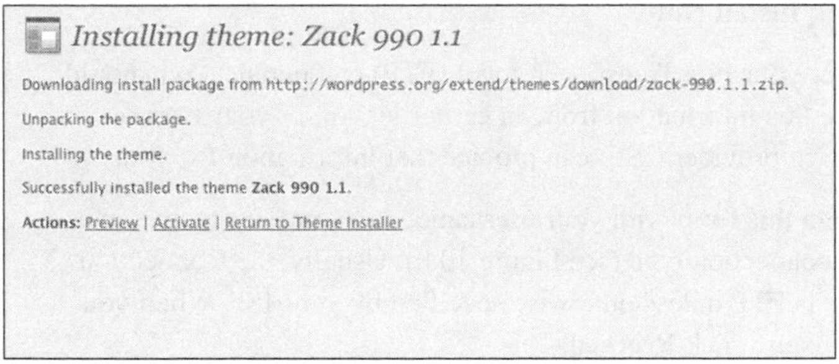

### Installing theme: Zack 990 1.1

Downloading install package from http://wordpress.org/extend/themes/download/zack-990.1.1.zip.

Unpacking the package.

Installing the theme.

Successfully installed the theme **Zack 990 1.1**.

**Actions:** Preview | Activate | Return to Theme Installer

**FIGURE 10.9**    WordPress's installation confirmation screen.

## Downloading and Installing Themes

If you do not have access to automatically install themes on your site, you have found a theme on another website, or you have purchased a premium theme, installing a theme is still easy.

NOTE: **Using FTP**

In this section, you access your site with an FTP client. If you don't
already have an FTP client, refer to Lesson 9, "Installing
WordPress," to find out more about using one.

On the WordPress.org themes site (http://wordpress.org/extend/themes),
select a theme that you think will work on your site and you are happy
with. After you choose a theme and are looking at its profile page (refer to
Figure 10.4), click on **Download**.

Most WordPress themes you download are in the form of a zip file that
you must save and unzip; this includes premium themes also. Your
browser asks you where you want to download your zip file. Save it to
a location on your computer that you will remember, such as a download
folder or your desktop.

When the download is complete, go to the folder where you downloaded
your theme. In that folder, you need to unzip your theme file; it creates a
folder. The folder it creates should be named the same as the theme. For
example, if your zip file is called AwesomeTheme-2.2.3.zip, your new
folder should be called AwesomeTheme.

Use your FTP client and connect to your hosting account. On the right
side of your client, you should see the remote files. Double-click on the
folder named wp-content. Now double-click on the folder named Themes.
You should see two folders: classic and default. These two standard
themes come with WordPress out of the box. The folder name's default is
the theme you see on your WordPress site as soon as the installation is
complete.

In the left pane of your FTP client, navigate to the download folder that
has the new theme you downloaded.

To upload your theme properly, upload the entire folder to your website.
In this example, you would upload AwesomeTheme to your site. After the
upload is complete, you should have three folders: classic, default, and
AwesomeTheme.

Now that your theme is uploaded, it's time to turn it on.

## Applying Themes

Changing between themes, now that they are installed, is fairly straight-forward.

1. Using your web browser, go to your Dashboard (http://www.yoursite.com/wp-admin).

2. On the left side of your Dashboard is a block called Appearance. Open that block and select Themes.

3. On the Managing Themes page, all the themes you have installed are listed. The theme listed at the top is your current one. Activate the theme you want to use by clicking the **Activate** link.

4. If you want to see how a theme is going to look before turning it on, click the **Preview** link or click the thumbnail.

   As you have seen before (refer to Figure 10.7), a preview appears. From the top-right corner of the preview, you can activate the theme if you are happy with its appearance.

---

TIP: **Deleting Themes**

If you have a theme you do not care for any longer, you can delete it from the Manage Themes page by clicking on **Delete** just below its description.

---

# Widgets

With your new theme installed and running, you might want to move things around a little bit. Perhaps you have a two- or three-column layout and want to move some of the items in those columns around a little bit or possibly put something in a column of your own. You can use widgets, which are similar to small plug-ins designed so that you can move them easily from place to place on your site, specifically in the sidebars.

From your Dashboard, go to **Appearance, Widgets**. On the resulting page, you see a list of available widgets in the center of the page and the columns available to your theme on the right (see Figure 10.10).

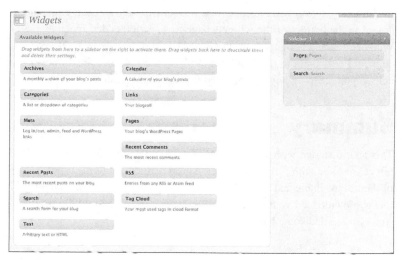

**FIGURE 10.10**    Available widgets with a one column theme.

Below each widget is a quick description of its function. To move a widget to a column—in this case, Sidebar 1—do the following:

1. Click your mouse on a widget and hold it.

2. Now drag and drop it over the column where you want it to appear.

3. When you drop the widget where you want it, usually it asks you for a title. This title is optional. If you want to call the Search widget Find It, for example, this is the place where you would assign it a name. Leave the field blank, and it defaults to the name of the widget.

Other widgets have more options than just the title. So be prepared if the one you choose asks for something more than just a title.

If you want to change a title or other options for a widget, click the small, downward-pointing arrow on the right of the title bar for the widget. It then expands, showing all the options available.

Additionally, if you want to remove a widget from the sidebar, click and drag it to the bottom of the widgets page to a section called Inactive Widgets. Placing widgets here removes them and their settings. If you click and drag them to the Available Widgets section, they are still available to you, keeping any settings that you may have added.

# Summary

This lesson started with a discussion of what themes are and how they affect your site with form and function. You learned about the types of themes available and their layouts. You also started with the default theme, downloaded your own, installed it, and customized it a little. You also learned some basic Widget skills.

# LESSON 11

# Customizing Your Site with Plug-ins

*Plug-ins make all the difference in how your WordPress.org site runs. This lesson discusses how you can use plug-ins to change the function of your self-hosted site and how to install some of the more popular plug-ins.*

## What Are Plug-ins?

In a nutshell, plug-ins are bits of code designed to extend the functionality of your site to do almost anything. WordPress itself is designed to be lean and functional out of the box, but with plug-ins you add the extra functionality you need. Everyone has different needs, so the capability to add plug-ins keeps the WordPress core code clean and uncluttered, while at the same time allowing you the flexibility to easily add on features that make your site what you need.

For example, if you want to create a podcasting site with WordPress, two plug-ins help with that task: PodPress and PowerPress. They provide similar functions. They take a link to an MP3 (your podcast file) and add a Flash Audio player on your site to each post with an MP3 link so you can play and listen to the episode and also add a download link and other information for your readers. These plug-ins also perform certain functions, such as notifying Apple iTunes that you have a new episode when you post one. With plug-ins, the possibilities for customizing your site become nearly endless.

# Using the Plug-ins Dashboard

The Plug-ins Dashboard is designed to give you complete access to manage the plug-ins installed on your site. From here you can install, activate, deactivate, and permantly remove plug-ins as you see fit. You can get to the Plug-ins Dashboard by opening your web browser and pointing it to your Dashboard (for example, http://www.yoursite.com/wp-admin). When you get there, click on **Plug-ins**. You then are presented with a list of all your plug-ins (see Figure 11.1). At this point, if you haven't added any plug-ins, you should see only two listed; they are the default plug-ins that come with WordPress: Akismet and Hello Dolly.

**FIGURE 11.1**   Plug-ins page displaying the default plug-ins.

This screen shows you all you need to know about your plug-ins. At the top, just below Manage Plug-ins, you may see several links that give you several group views of all your plug-ins and each link allows you to toggle between the category groupings. The categories are as follows:

▶ **All** displays all the plug-ins you have installed.

▶ **Active** displays all the plug-ins you have installed and currently in use on your site.

▶ **Inactive** shows a list of plug-ins you have available on the system but not currently activated.

▶ **Upgrade Available** gives you a list of plug-ins you have on the
   system that need an upgrade. Plug-in authors release upgrades to
   plug-ins when adding new features or possibly addressing security issues.

▶ **Recently Active** shows the plug-ins you recently deactivated.
   This list is handy if you accidentally deactivate a plug-in and
   need to quickly turn it back on.

---

NOTE: **Some Categories Are Missing**

You may not see all these categories until you start adding some
plug-ins or depending on the state of your plug-ins. For example, if
you don't have any plug-ins that need an upgrade, you do not see
the Upgrade Available view, or you may not see Inactive if all your
plug-ins are active.

---

All your plug-ins are listed in the middle portion of the page. Each one
displays its name and a description. Just below the name and description
are Activate and Delete links for each one. If a plug-in is already activated, you see Deactivate instead. To the right of the Activate, Delete, and
Deactivate links are the current version of the plug-in and possibly links
to the author and the plug-in's site.

To the left of each plug-in listed is a check box. The check boxes are used
in conjunction with the Bulk Actions list box. If you select all the plug-ins
or a couple, you can then select an action from the list and perform that
action on all selected plug-ins. This capability can save time if you are
changing the status of several plug-ins at once.

---

CAUTION: **Deleting Permanently**

Deleting a plug-in *permanently* removes all the files associated with
the plug-in. If you do not want use a plug-in now and possibly try it
later, I suggest just deactivating it. If plug-ins are cluttering your
workspace and you don't plan on using them anymore, there is nothing wrong with deleting old plug-ins.

---

Below the Plug-ins menu item are the following options:

▶ **Installed** takes you to a list of all installed plug-ins (active or inactive), or if upgrades are available, this option takes you to the list of plug-ins that have an upgrade available.

▶ **Add New** takes you to the search screen to start looking for plug-ins that you might want to install. This option allows you to search the list of plug-ins available on the WordPress plug-ins directory, directly from your WordPress site. (More details on this in the next part of this lesson.)

▶ **Editor** lets you edit the code of your plug-ins. If you're not familiar with PHP, you might not need to use the editor.

> NOTE: **File Permissions for Plug-ins**
>
> To edit files properly and be able to save them, you might need to check your file permissions on the files to make sure you have access to write to them.

> CAUTION: **Be Careful When Editing**
>
> Editing your plug-ins can cause them to become unstable unless you know what you are changing. Use the Editor option with caution.

# Finding Plug-ins

There are several places to start your search for WordPress plug-ins, and I recommend starting with the "official" plug-ins repository for a couple of reasons.

Anyone can submit a plug-in for inclusion in this repository, but not all will be listed. A few restrictions and standards must be met for inclusion in the plug-ins repository:

▶ The plug-in must be GPL-compatible. This means, in the simplest terms, you are free to download and use the plug-in. If you modify it and release it as a new plug-in, you must release it under the same license.

▶ The plug-in must not do anything illegal or immoral.

▶ The plug-in cannot add any external links unless the user explicitly gives permission to do so.

These restrictions as well as other standards that WordPress enforces only make your decision a little easier if you choose plug-ins from the WordPress repository:

▶ There is no cost, and licensing isn't an issue.

▶ You can modify the code if you want with no restrictions if you have some programming skills or know someone who does.

▶ These plug-ins do not have malicious code that can be harmful to your site.

If you do not find the plug-ins you are looking for here, there are other alternatives. Simply search for "WordPress plug-in" on Google or your favorite search engine, and you will find a lot of other sites that also host WordPress plug-ins. Keep in mind that much of what you are looking for can be found in the WordPress repository.

---

CAUTION: **Not All Plug-ins Are Created Equal**

Take caution where you download plug-ins from. The plug-ins are just PHP code that can do anything, even something malicious. So, download with care.

---

As with themes, premium plug-ins are also available for a fee. There are not as many premium plug-ins as there are premium themes, but this is starting to become a larger business. The main advantage for you is if you are looking for support in the form of someone to contact in case you need installation help or modifications. Costs can range from $4 to more than $60. Again, at the time of this writing, there are a lot more free plug-ins than premium.

Because there are so many places from which you could possibly download WordPress plug-ins, I focus on the Official WordPress repository here. Keep in mind that wherever you download plug-ins, the basic steps are the same.

There are two ways to access the plug-ins directory at WordPress: You can access plug-ins from the WordPress Dashboard or by visiting http://wordpress.org/extend/plug-ins/.

> NOTE: **Writing Your Own Plug-in**
>
> You can write your own plug-in or hire someone to write a plug-in for you. Writing plug-ins is not difficult if you have some programming skills, some knowledge of PHP, and some extra time. Writing plug-ins for WordPress is very well documented on the WordPress site as well as other sites across the Internet.
>
> However, lots of plug-ins are already available, and likely there is one already written that does what you need. So be sure to do a thorough search first because it could save you time in the long run.

## Searching from Your Dashboard

To search from the Dashboard, click on **Plug-ins**, **Add New**. If you are viewing your plug-ins from the Managing Plug-ins page, you also can click the **Add New** button at the top of the page. It takes you to the same search page.

At the top of the Install Plug-ins page is a list of views that will assist you in finding and installing plug-ins:

- ▶ **Search** allows you to search through the plug-ins directory on the WordPress site and also allows you to navigate through all the plug-ins via the tags assigned to them—for example, Comments, Twitter, and Stats.

- ▶ **Upload** walks you through uploading a zip file that contains a plug-in that you downloaded manually.

- ▶ **Featured** shows you the plug-ins showcased by WordPress. They are chosen based on user activity and popularity.

- ▶ **Popular** highlights the plug-ins with the highest ratings and number of users.

- ▶ **Newest** shows the newest plug-ins added recently to the directory.

▶ **Recently Updated** also shows the plug-ins recently updated either for functionality or security reasons.

Click on **Search**, and you see the page shown in Figure 11.2.

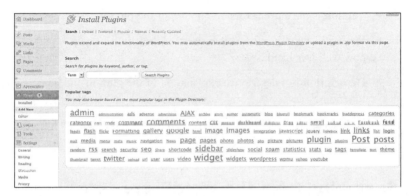

**FIGURE 11.2**   Starting the search for plug-ins.

On the Install Plug-ins page, you are presented with a search box where you can search for plug-ins by keyword, author, or *tag*. Also, you are presented with a *tag cloud* full of keywords that you can click on and instantly find plug-ins associated with the tag you choose.

PLAIN ENGLISH: **Tag**

A *tag* is a word or set of words associated with an item that helps identify it. In this instance, tags are associated with plug-ins. A *tag cloud* is a view of all the tags in the database. In the tag cloud, larger and bolder tags represent more items, and smaller, less bold tags indicate fewer items.

Type in a search word or click on a tag word from the tag cloud. You then are presented with a list of plug-ins that match your search results in a grid list. This list is composed of five columns:

- **Name** is, of course, the name of the plug-in.
- **Version** is the current version number of the plug-in.
- **Rating** is the rating from other users of this plug-in indicating how well it is liked.
- **Description** is a descriptive explanation of the plug-in and its functions.
- **Actions** shows what functions you can take on the plug-ins listed, and it will say **Install**.

## Searching from the WordPress Site

Searching for plug-ins on the WordPress repository site is similar, but results are displayed a little differently (see Figure 11.3).

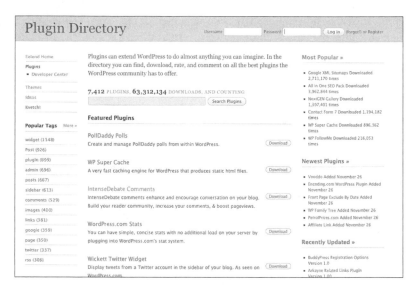

**FIGURE 11.3** Searching for plug-ins on the WordPress repository site.

On the left side of the site, below the links to other places on the site, is the title Popular Tags. This is a shorthand representation of the tag cloud. You can see the popular tags and the number of plug-ins associated with them. Clicking **More** shows you the tag cloud much like you saw in your Dashboard.

Among other features here, again mimicking Dashboard searching, is a search box in the center with Featured Plug-ins below. To the right are Most Popular, Newest Plug-ins, and Recently Updated.

If you choose to install from the WordPress site, you have to download the plug-in yourself and upload it to your site using the automated instal lation functions of WordPress or the manual installation method using your FTP client.

When you find a plug-in that you would like to use and are looking at its profile on Wordpress.org, you see the orange Download button. When you click **Download**, you are asked to download a zip file. After you download it, note where you saved it.

# Installing a Plug-in

There are several things you should know before you start installing plug-ins:

- ▶ Some plug-ins require changes to permissions of files and folders on your website.

- ▶ Some plug-ins may require changes or additions to your site's themes to work properly.

- ▶ You should make backups of your site's files and its database. If you lose the files and database and don't have a backup, you lose your website.

---

TIP: **Good Practices for Editing Code**

If you're a programmer who is making modifications to your theme or other files, follow these guidelines for good code management: Put in a comment with your initials and a date so you will know what you changed. Also, avoid deleting lines but use comments in the code to hide old lines. Or simply copy the file you are about to edit and rename it for easy identification if you need to roll back a change.

Generally, there are three methods for installing plug-ins. They are described next.

## Fully Automatic

The easiest way to install plug-ins is to use the fully automatic option. If you have searched for a plug-in through your Dashboard, an Install link (mentioned previously) appears in orange.

After you click **Install**, you are asked for your FTP credentials much like you have seen previously in other lessons. After you fill out the form, click **Proceed**. If all works correctly, you see a status page with the option to activate the plug-in right away, or you can choose to go back to the plug-ins page and activate it later (see Figure 11.4).

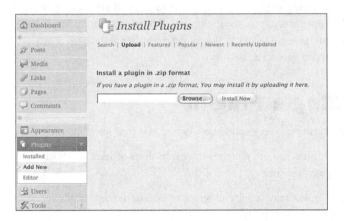

**FIGURE 11.4**   Installing from a zip file.

---

NOTE: **Folder Permissions**

If you get an error installing from the WordPress Dashboard, your permissions may not be set correctly on your web server. If you do not know how to set permissions on folders, contact your web hosting support for assistance.

# Automated Installation

If you choose not to use the fully automatic installation method, or you are installing a plug-in that you got from somewhere other than the official WordPress repository, the steps to install it are nearly as easy.

1. Open your web browser and navigate to your Dashboard; then go to **Plug-ins, Add New**.

2. On the Dashboard page, below the title **Install Plug-ins** at the top of the page, notice the Upload option to the left of Search. Upload takes your zip file, copies it to the web server, expands it, and places all its files into the correct place.

3. Click **Browse**. Navigate to the download folder where you placed your plug-in zip file and select the zip file to upload. When you have the filename in place, click the **Install Now** button.

4. You are prompted for your FTP credentials. Make sure these fields are correct and click **Proceed**.

5. If the upload performs correctly, you see page that displays the status of what is occurring or has occurred with a link to a couple of actions. You can immediately activate your new plug-in from here or simply return to the plug-ins page if you are not ready to take action on your new plug-in (see Figure 11.5).

You can activate your new plug-in later if you choose, but it is installed and ready to use now.

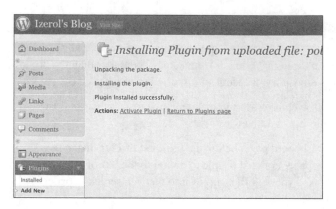

**FIGURE 11.5**    Installation complete.

# Manual Installation

The zip file that you downloaded is the plug-in itself. To proceed, you
need to upload the plug-in files to your webserver:

1. Go to your download folder where you saved the plug-in and
   expand the zip file.

2. Once expanded, the zip file is ready for upload. Open your FTP
   program and log in to your site.

3. After you open it, navigate to the wp-contents folder, where you
   see a plug-ins folder. Open the plug-ins folder and upload your
   expanded plug-in zip file here.

4. After you successfully upload your plug-in into the wp-content,
   plug-ins directory, you need to activate your plug-in by visiting
   your Dashboard at http://yoursite.com/wp-admin and click on
   **Plug-ins**.

5. On the plug-ins page, an additional link called **Inactive** appears
   just below the Manage Plug-ins title.

6. If you click on **Inactive**, you see all the plug-ins that you currently do not have enabled. The new plug-in you uploaded is
   shown here. As you did earlier with the Hello Dolly plug-in,
   click **Activate** below Title on the plug-in column.

That's it. Your new plug-in is now activated.

# Upgrading Plug-ins

As time goes on, upgrades, security releases, or new features will be added to the plug-ins that you accumulate. It is important that you are able to keep up and make sure that your system is up to date.

There are several reasons for keeping your code up to date, and chief among them is security of your site. Plus, upgrading plug-ins is not as hard as you may think.

One of the advantages of downloading your plug-ins from the WordPress repository is that your copy of WordPress will let you know that upgrades are available. This is not true of plug-ins you have downloaded from other sites.

Two notifications alert you that updates are available. On the menu to the left in your WordPress Dashboard, notice that the Plug-ins menu header has a number highlighted in a circle (see Figure 11.6). This circle shows you the number of updates you have.

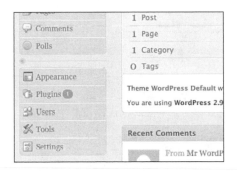

**FIGURE 11.6**   Upgrades available.

Additionally, if you visit your plug-ins page by clicking on **Plug-ins**, each plug-in that has an update available has a highlighted area associated with it that gives you a little information about the update.

If you click on **Details**, you see a pop-up window much like you saw when searching for plug-ins with details on the update and an **Install Update Now** option. If you click on **ChangeLog** at the top of the pop-up window, you see a list of changes that have been implemented since the last released version.

> NOTE: **Check ChangeLog**
>
> I recommend looking at the ChangeLog to see if the changes being made will affect any of the reasons you use this plug-in. It is good to be aware of what is happening in case questions come up later.

After you click on **Install Update Now**, you are asked to confirm your connection information with your FTP credentials. Fill out this page and click **Proceed**.

The next page shows you the progress as it downloads the plug-in and upgrades the code (see Figure 11.7).

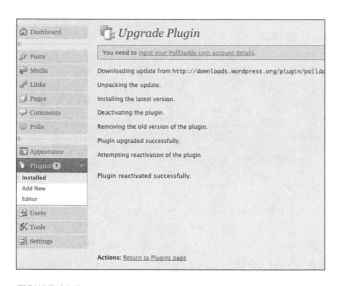

**FIGURE 11.7**   Upgrade complete.

> NOTE: **Notification Reminders**
>
> Plug-ins you have installed that are not in the WordPress repository do not notify you that you have updates waiting.

# Removing a Plug-in

It is inevitable that eventually you will have plug-ins you no longer use and want to disable or even delete entirely. This is very common, so WordPress makes it simple to remove old plug-ins.

1. Navigate to the Plug-ins panel in your Dashboard

2. Under the title Manage Plug-ins is your list of plug-ins. Under the plug-in you want to remove, you should see the Deactivate button.

3. Click **Deactivate** and you will then see two new options: Activate and Delete.

4. After a plug-in is deactivated, you can remove it for permanently by clicking **Delete**.

5. You are taken to a Delete Plug-in confirmation page. From here, if you choose **Yes, Delete These Files**, your plug-in is removed from your website permanently.

If you select **No, Return Me to the Plug-in List**, nothing happens, but you are returned to the plug-in list. Your plug-in will still be there if you choose to activate it later.

> CAUTION: **Deactivate and then Delete**
>
> Keep in mind that some, not all, plug-ins have dependencies on others. Deactivating one and deleting it may have adverse effects on your site. I recommend deactivating first; then check your site to make sure it is in good shape and delete only after you verify everything is okay.

# Popular Plug-ins

Following are some popular plug-ins that you might find useful. They are all found in the WordPress.org plug-ins directory.

## Ads

▶ **Google Adsense for feeds**—This plug-in puts Google RSS ads in your feed. Make sure you fill in your publisher ID by editing the plug-in file.

▶ **Advertising Manager**—This plug-in manages and rotates Google Adsense and other ads on your Wordpress blog. It automatically recognizes many ad networks, including Google Adsense, AdBrite, Adify, AdGridWork, Adpinion, Adroll, Chitika, Commission Junction, CrispAds, OpenX, ShoppingAds, Yahoo!PN, and WidgetBucks. Unsupported ad networks can be used as well.

## Spam

▶ **Akismet**—This default plug-in is available in your WordPress site. This plug-in helps curb spam by comparing it to a database of other spam messages that WordPress.com collects to determine if it is in fact spam. (This plug-in requires a WordPress.com account.)

▶ **WP-SpamFree Anti-Spam**—This extremely powerful WordPress antispam plug-in eliminates blog comment spam, including trackback and pingback spam.

## Getting the Word Out

▶ **Wp-pubsubhubbub**—This plug-in contacts and sends notification of changes on your site to pubsubhubbub hubs so that new posts are known and available to search engines.

# Statistics

▶ **Wordpress.com Stats**—This plug-in was created by the company Automattic to collect your site's visitor data and statistics to create easy-to-understand graphs and dates of your site's visitation traffic. (This plug-in requires a WordPress.com account.)

▶ **Google Analyticator**—This plug-in adds the necessary JavaScript code to enable Google Analytics to keep statistics on visitors to your site. It includes widgets for Analytics data display.

# Social Networking

▶ **Sociable**—This plug-in enables you to automatically add links to your favorite social bookmarking sites on your posts, pages, and in your RSS feed. You can choose from 99 different social bookmarking sites.

▶ **Social Bookmarks**— This plug-in for WordPress adds a list of XHTML-compliant graphic links at the end of your posts and/or pages. These links allow your visitors to easily submit them to a number of social bookmarking sites.

▶ **Twitter Tools**—This plug-in creates a complete integration between your WordPress blog and your Twitter account.

# Podcasting

▶ **Blubrry PowerPress**—This plug-in brings the essential features for podcasting to WordPress. Developed by podcasters for podcasters, PowerPress offers full iTunes support, the Update iTunes Listing feature, web audio/video media players, and more. PowerPress is designed as an upgrade to PodPress.

# Summary

In this lesson, you learned what plug-ins are and what they do. You also explored the Plug-ins Dashboard and used the search functions in WordPress to find and install plug-ins using the fully automatic, automated installation, and manual methods. Finally, you looked at the process of upgrading and removing old plug-ins.

# Blogging on the Go

*You can't always be on your computer. With a smart phone and the avail-ability of Wi-Fi, you can take the blogging experience with you almost anywhere you go. There are several ways to get posts to your blog, from email to iPhone apps. This lesson describes the various ways you can blog on the go.*

## Setting Up Your Blog for Remote Access

Blogging can be fun, and with wireless technology there's no reason you can't do it while you are out and about. Perhaps you are at a conference or on a special vacation, and you would like to blog about your experi-ences as they happen. WordPress can make that a very real possibility. Capturing your thoughts and blogging them right away can be very capti-vating for readers of your site.

To remotely access your blog, you have to turn on the WordPress feature to allow outside applications to connect and interact with your site. By default, this feature is turned off. There are two ways that outside applica-tions can interact with WordPress:

▶ Atom Publishing

▶ XML-RPC

---

NOTE: **WordPress.com Versus WordPress.org**

If you are using a WordPress.com account, the Remote Publishing feature is turned on by default as opposed to your WordPress.org install.

---

Use the following steps to turn on an option for remote access:

1. Open your site's Dashboard.

2. Select **Settings, Writing**.

3. In the Remote Publishing section, select the **XML-RPC** option.

4. Click **Save Changes**.

---

CAUTION: **Enable Only What You Need**

I recommend turning on only the options you believe you are going to use. Turning on features you are not using could be a security risk.

---

NOTE: **XML-RPC or Atom Publishing?**

I cannot say that one publishing protocol is better than another; however, the applications that are discussed in this lesson support XML-RPC for remote operations, so that's the protocol used in this lesson. Of course, if you come across an application that supports Atom Publishing, you can come back here and easily turn it on.

---

Now, to use your remote blogging capabilities, you need to know only your site's URL, username, and password, and you are set.

---

NOTE: **Finding the XML-RPC Script**

Some sites and applications are smart enough to figure out where your XML-RPC script is, and others want a complete URL to your site, including the XML-RPC script. If that is the case, use http://www.yoursite.com/xml-rpc.php instead of http://www.yoursite.com.

# Posting from Other Websites

Some websites offer interaction with other sites using remote publishing. This can be very beneficial by allowing you to create more compelling content on your site by including material from other places across the internet.

## Flickr

Flickr, a popular photo-sharing site, offers support for a variety of websites.

Say you upload a picture from your camera phone to Flickr, and you want to also post that image on your blog. Flickr allows you to set up several blogs to publish to, not just one.

> NOTE: **Flickr Accounts**
>
> To use Flickr to post photos, you need a Flickr account. It is free, and you get a generous amount of space to store images. Flickr does offer Pro accounts with a few more features and more storage space.

1. After you set up your Flickr account and are logged in, click the arrow directly to the right of **You** and select **Your Account**.

2. Now you see a tab labeled Extending Flickr, Click it.

3. On that tab, you see Your Blogs, Click it.

4. Click the **Configure-Flickr-to-Blogs Setting** link.

5. Flickr walks you through the process with a wizard that will eventually ask for your URL, username, and password.

After you configure your blog, you can go directly back to the same location and edit the settings for your blog, including the default layout, and even post a test post.

The layout allows you to set the default image site and text flow, so it looks correct on your blog each time (see Figure 12.1).

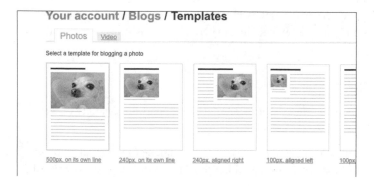

**FIGURE 12.1**    Using Flickr to configure the default layout of your blog.

After you set up your blog, above any picture in your photostream that you have marked as public is a **Blog This** icon. The Blog This icon is also available for any photo that is on Flickr that is marked as public and the photographer has allowed allow blogging of his or her photos.

After you click **Blog This**, as shown in Figure 12.2, Flickr asks which blog (you can configure more than one) and prompts you for a title and text body. After you submit this information, it is published to your site.

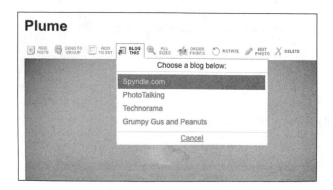

**FIGURE 12.2**    Blogging a picture from Flickr.

# Posterous

The Posterous service enables you to send emails to your Posterous account, and it creates a blog for you. Posterous not only creates a blog for you (non-WordPress), but also directs your messages to several services on your behalf, including Twitter, Facebook, WordPress, and others.

The Posterous page tells you that you don't have to set up an account to start using the services; however, to add your WordPress blog for posting, you need to set up one.

To set up a page, visit the Posterous site at http://posterous.com and click on the login in the top-right corner.

1. You can create an account using your Facebook credentials if you want or click on the **Sign up with Posterous** button.

2. The service asks what you want your site's name to be and your email address (for your account login) and a password. When this setup is complete, you can email post@posterous.com, and the service routes your message wherever you have it set to go.

3. After creating your account, log in. You see Manage at the top of the page. From there, you can set up where your messages will be routed.

Setting up WordPress autoposting is easy.

1. Click on the **Autopost** heading on the left side.

2. Click on the large green **Add a Service** button (see Figure 12 3). The resulting pop-up shows you all the services that Posterous uses.

3. In the Blogs section on the pop-up window, select **WordPress**, and you are presented with the familiar settings that you have been using, including your site's URL, username, and password.

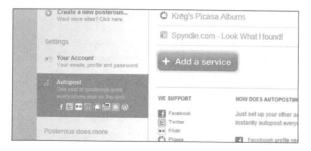

**FIGURE 12.3**  Setting up autoposting in Posterous.

---

NOTE: **Post to Multiple Sites with Posterous**

What is nice about Posterous is that anything you send in is sent to all the services you have set up. So, one post is posted to many sites, or Posterous can provide you with a special email address so you can post to just one site at a time.

---

Now you are all set. You can post text, pictures, and video to your WordPress site and other services, all at the same time, through one email message.

# Using Mobile Applications

There are lots of mobile applications for either the iPhone or BlackBerry. There are also applications for other mobile devices, such as Android, but not an official one as of yet. Here we focus on the Official WordPress application written by Automattic, Inc., the company behind WordPress.

There are versions for the iPhone and the BlackBerry; they both work similarly and both support a WordPress.com account as well as your own self-hosted WordPress.org site.

## Using the iPhone App

The WordPress application is available through the App Store. You can install it by opening the App Store and searching for WordPress. The App Store walks you through the installation process.

To configure the iPhone app with your first blog:

1. Click on the app's icon to open it.

2. You are prompted for your username, password, and URL.

3. After you have entered your credentials, click **Save**.

4. A pop-up window tells you that the app is being validated. Let the validation process complete.

5. After the app is installed, you see content from your site starting with comments.

Now that you are viewing your blog, at the top left of the screen is a link to go back to your blog's list, and a button on the right has an edit button (see Figure 12.4). This is the place where you make new posts.

**FIGURE 12.4**    WordPress functions on the iPhone and iPod touch.

At the bottom, you see three buttons:

▶ **Comments**—Allows you to moderate comments as they come in

▶ **Posts**—Enables you to create and edit posts

▶ **Pages**—Enables you to create pages on your site

You can perform any blogging function from this application. Creating a post is intuitive. You can even add media; for example, you can upload pictures that you have taken with your cell phone camera or even take one at that moment.

Clicking Blogs will take you back to your Blog List. An Edit button appears at the top left, and a + button is on the right (see Figure 12.5).

Clicking **Edit** changes to edit mode and allows you to delete any blogs that you have listed, and clicking + prompts you to add a new blog, if you have another to add. While in Edit mode, you can click on your blog and change any settings for it, such as your username and password.

**FIGURE 12.5**   Using your blog on your iPhone or iPod touch.

If you're not in Edit mode, clicking on the blog's title takes you to the screen where you can view the content and work with your selected blog.

## BlackBerry

If you are a BlackBerry user, an application is also available for that platform.

> CAUTION: Something to keep in mind before you install the BlackBerry app is that at press time of this book, the Blackberry application is in beta and not a final release version. Options and features could change by the time you read this and, as with all beta/pre-release software, you should be aware that you could run into bugs that might cause you trouble.

To install the BlackBerry application:

1. Open your web browser and navigate to http://blackberry.word-press.org.

2. Click the download link on the top-right side.

3. Your BlackBerry asks if you want to install the application and walks you through the rest of the installation process.

After installing the BlackBerry application, you can start adding blogs that you write for and start posting.

The main difference between this and the iPhone application is that the BlackBerry relies on the context menu (by clicking the BlackBerry Menu button) to perform many of its functions.

To start adding a blog, click the BlackBerry Menu button. You then can perform several functions:

▶ **Show Blog**—Shows you the options for the blog you have high-lighted (if you already have one set up on the main page).

▶ **Add Blog**—Allows you to create and set up a blog for posting or managing.

▶ **Delete Blog**—Will remove a blog that you have highlighted (if you already have one set up on the main page).

▶ **Setup**—Allows you to set various options regarding how this application talks to the Internet and so on. Most likely, the defaults will work for you.

▶ **Check Update**—Checks to see whether you have an update to your WordPress mobile application.

▶ **About**—Displays version and other information about this appli-cation.

Select **Add Blog**. You are asked for the familiar credentials described ear-lier in the lesson. Once set, your BlackBerry application tries to authenti-cate you and download information, such as the last 10 posts and any comments that need approving.

Now you are set and ready to blog from your BlackBerry. You can add posts and media from your cell phone's camera and moderate comments as you would on your blog from your computer.

> TIP: **Why Can't I See My Posts?**
> If posts have been made since you last opened your BlackBerry application—for example, posts you made from your computer—you might have to click the **Refresh** menu option to see the newer posts (see Figure 12.6).

**FIGURE 12.6**   WordPress functions for a blog on the BlackBerry.

# Using Email to Post

I like to blog from my mobile device, but there are some issues to consider when you do so, especially while you're on vacation. Usually I vacation with my family, and they tend to frown on my monkeying around on my BlackBerry. And to be honest, trying to make a quick post with the

BlackBerry, iPhone, or iPod Touch using the mobile applications can take a little longer than shooting off an email.

The mobile apps are great, but sending an email to your blog can be a quick and effective way to blog. You can add pictures or media, and everything is picked up on the other end. This approach is quicker and less cumbersome and will score some points with whomever you are vacationing with.

# Email Posting with WordPress.com

If you want to set up your WordPress.com blog for email posting, visit WordPress.com and log in with your account.

1.  Along the menu at the top of your screen, click **My Dashboards** to see a drop-down menu with all the blogs you have configured.

2.  At the bottom, click **Manage Blogs**.

3.  You now see a page titled Blogs You're a Member Of.

4.  To the right is a column called Post by Email. For each blog listed, you see an Enable button.

5.  Clicking **Enable** generates a secret email address for your blog.

That's it; now you're ready to post by email to your WordPress.com blog.

> TIP: **My Secret Email Isn't Secret Anymore!**
> If you hover your mouse cursor over the email address, you see the Regenerate and Delete options. If your secret email address becomes public, or you need to change it for another reason, you can regenerate it by clicking **Regenerate**, and you create a completely new address to post to.

# Email Posting with WordPress.org

To set up your WordPress.org blog for email posting:

1.  Open your Dashboard in your web browser and navigate to **Settings**, **Writing**.

2. You then see a section called Post via E-mail. It is recommended that you create a special email address to use as your publishing email.

   You can create an email address for posting to your blog through your web host, or you can create one through one of the free email services offered by Yahoo!, Google, and others.

---

CAUTION: **Don't Share This Email Address**

WordPress recommends posting via email using an email address that is secret—for example, hr22ma@yourdomain.com. It is a good idea not to share this email address with anyone because anyone who has the address is able to post to your blog.

---

3. After you have your secret email address, you need the URL of the email server, your username, and your password to proceed (see Figure 12.7).

---

TIP: **SSL on Email Servers**

Some services, such as Google's Gmail, use SSL to secure your connection to your email. If you use a service that requires SSL, you might have to indicate that as part of the email server's URL—for example, ssl://pop.gmail.com (see Figure 12.7).

---

**Post via e-mail**

To post to WordPress by e-mail you must set up a secret e-mail account with POP3 access. Any mail received at this address will
very secret. Here are three random strings you could use: W1iKx2SA , GRDHCcd4 , mQlhgtYS .

| | | |
|---|---|---|
| Mail Server | ssl://pop.gmail.com | Port 995 |
| Login Name | SuperSecret@gmail.com | |
| Password | MyPassWord | |
| Default Mail Category | General ▾ | |

**FIGURE 12.7**   Settings for email publishing.

4. After filling out your information, click **Save Changes**.

There is one caveat with posting in this manner: When you are running your own WordPress.org site much like you have to check your email, your WordPress blog has to check for email, too. Unfortunately, this process is not automatic. Each time you send an email to your secret email address, you have to visit the URL http://yourdomain.com/wp-mail.php for it to pick up your posts.

For WordPress.com sites, this is automatic.

This procedure can be automated with a CRON job for your WordPress.org site. CRON is a UNIX application that runs jobs at a certain time and date of your choosing. Some web hosts allow you to create a CRON job and automate the process of having WordPress check for messages.

---

**CAUTION: Setting the Frequency of CRON Jobs**

Don't set your CRON job to have WordPress check your email too often. Some email providers may frown on that. I recommend setting up your CRON job to check once an hour or perhaps twice a day, depending on your expected use.

---

Now that you have your settings in place, you are ready to email your blog messages and pictures as you travel around.

---

**NOTE: Formatting in Emails**

If you send emails with HTML formatting, be aware that Wordpress.com and .org strip unnecessary HTML from your messages while retaining some of the formatting. When your emails appear on your blog, they might not look exactly as you created them.

Also, be aware that any email signature you have on your outgoing email (including disclaimers) could show up on your blog posts.

# Using ScribeFire

ScribeFire is a free plug-in for Firefox that allows you to post directly from your web browser. If you're wondering why you would use a plug-in instead of just using the Dashboard to make a post, the reason is that ScribeFire makes it extra easy to reference other pages or blog posts in posts you write. You can cut and paste from the page you are viewing, as well as create links and add pictures from the plug-in, all without having to open your blog to switch between tabs or open windows to gather your information.

To install ScribeFire in Firefox, visit the plug-in's page at http://scribefire.com.

1. On the right side of the page, click the **Install ScribeFire Now** link. This link takes you to the ScribeFire page at the Firefox Add-ons page.

2. Click on the **Add to Firefox** button, and Firefox walks you through the rest of the process. If you have installed plug-ins previously in Firefox, this process will be familiar.

3. After the plug-in is installed, an orange icon appears on the bottom-right side of Firefox's status bar (see Figure 12.8).

4. Clicking this icon opens a window that overlays about one third of the viewing area of your browser.

**JRE 12.8**    The ScribeFire button in Firefox.

This window should look familiar in the sense that there is an editor in which you can view the WYSIWYG editor, the source, or a preview of what your post will look like.

On the right side is a button labeled Launch Account Wizard. If this is your first time running ScribeFire, the wizard might start automatically. If not, click Launch Account Wizard, and ScribeFire walks you through the process of adding your blog or blogs. First, you add your blog's URL and click **Continue**.

The wizard identifies the software you are using for your blog; in this case, it is WordPress. The wizard also automatically supplies the API URL. Click **Continue** again. Then you are asked for the username and password for your blog. After entering this information, click **Continue**.

The wizard logs in to your website and then asks you to confirm the addition. Click **Continue**. On the last wizard screen, ScribeFire tells you it has added the account. Click **Done**. Now you are ready to blog from ScribeFire.

---

NOTE: **Adding More Than One Blog**

If you have more than one blog you want to configure, clicking the **Add** button below your list of blogs also launches the Account Wizard.

---

Before you create a post, look at the options on the right. Clicking on the orange ScribeFire icon opens an area on the right with tabs. These tabs are as follows:

▶ **Blogs**—Provides a list of all the blogs you have configured.

▶ **Entries**—Offers you a view into the content on your site. There are three tabs under the Entries tab: Posts, Notes, and Pages. This is content on your site. You can select any of these tabs and edit your content directly from here without having to visit your site's Dashboard.

▶ **Categories**—Lists all the categories you have configured on your site for your content. ScribeFire reads them in and makes them available for you to use as you create posts. It also lists your tags at the bottom.

▶ **Options**—Provides options for the post you are creating; for example, you can change some of the settings, including changing the time stamp of a post so it will show in the future. You can also set tags and turn on pinging if you want.

To create a post, you can just open ScribeFire by clicking the orange icon in Firefox (refer to Figure 12.8). You can also right-click on a page in Firefox that you want to reference, and you can use the ScribeFire options in the context menu.

Try opening any web page and highlighting some text. Then right-click and select **Blog This Page** (see Figure 12.9). ScribeFire opens, and a link to the blog is created with the text that you highlighted shown in the editor.

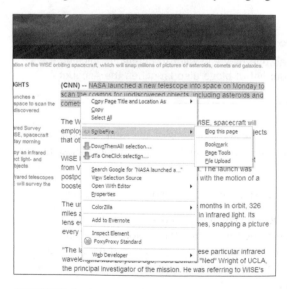

**FIGURE 12.9**   Using the context menu to blog about the page you are on.

From here, you can add your own commentary into your post, or you can cut and paste more quotes from the page you are viewing.

After you create your post and are happy with it, be sure to assign it a category. On the right side is a tab called Categories, beside the Entries tab. This is a list of the categories you have on your site set up for categorizing your posts.

Click **Publish to (Your Blog)**, and a small pop-up window asks if you want to publish as new posts or page. Select the appropriate choice for your post, normally **Post**. Then click **Publish**. When the item is successfully published, click **OK** to clear the editor. Alternatively, you can click **Keep Content** or **View this Blog**. When finished, close the window.

You can also save a draft of your post if you like. Select the check box, and when you publish as a draft, the post is not live, but you can edit it and continue with it later from your Entries, Posts tab (see Figure 12.10) or from your WordPress Dashboard. Drafts are shown in Red.

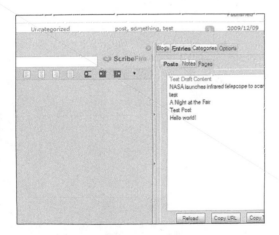

**FIGURE 12.10**   Viewing existing content and drafts in ScribeFire.

> NOTE: **Editing in ScribeFire**
>
> If you are editing content that already exists, you see the pop-up windows that ask you whether you want to post as an edit.

ScribeFire provides many more options, including using bookmarking services to share content with other social networks, creating notes for research on posts you want to make, and uploading media to your site.

# Summary

In this lesson, you discovered how powerful remote publishing to WordPress can be, yet this lesson only scratched the surface with a few convenient services and applications. You set up WordPress to allow remote publishing, configured it to accept email submissions, and configured several websites to interact with your site, making publishing easy and flexible for yourself.

# LESSON 13
# WordPress Support

*Sometimes you might have to look for help while working with WordPress. The knowledge of friends and family may take you only so far. In this lesson, you look at the various support options you have with WordPress whether you self-host or use WordPress.com.*

## Looking for Help

WordPress is open source software. It is free for you to download and use, and you can even modify the code for your needs. As is the nature of open source software, you can find help in a many places.

One advantage of WordPress support is that it has such a large user base; therefore, it is inevitable that someone else has had the same problem as you and has already solved it. Because WordPress is a blogging tool, often you will find that people post their solutions to problems through their blogs.

Blogs are not the only area for help with WordPress. There are many free support channels, and there are those you can pay for and be able to contact someone.

## Free Support

You can find free support for WordPress in many different formats, such as using WordPress documentation, searching the Internet, and reading WordPress forums.

# WordPress Documentation

Before you start searching the Internet high and low for instructions on how to do something, consulting the WordPress.org documentation is a good place to start. Visit http://codex.wordpress.org to read the documentation.

The official WordPress documentation is very well organized and well written. It is a *wiki* that is set up so that anyone can add documentation; you get input from a lot of sources on how things work with WordPress. The reason it is such a good resource is that you get input from lots of individuals. If you have knowledge about a particular subject and you would like to share, you, too, can participate. To do so, just create an account at http://codex.wordpress.org.

> PLAIN ENGLISH: **Wiki**
>
> A wiki is a website set up so that anyone can view and edit the information on the site. This capability might sound strange at first, but wikis have real value. If you come to a wiki such as this, you can add information that you know about and someone else can do the same. Eventually, you have knowledge from several sources and a quality set of source material.

The WordPress documentation is organized from beginner topics to advanced.

- ▶ Getting Started with WordPress—Installing and upgrading WordPress
- ▶ WordPress 2.9 Information—Compatibility, feature lists, and so on
- ▶ Working with WordPress—Administration, themes, plug-ins, and spam
- ▶ Design and Layout—Installing and creating themes
- ▶ Advanced Topics—WordPress MU (multiuser), backing up
- ▶ Troubleshooting—Support forms and FAQs
- ▶ Developer Documentation—How-to documentation on creating themes and plug-ins

- About WordPress—General information about WordPress

A lot of information is available in the WordPress documentation. As you grow and learn more about WordPress, this should be your first resource online.

## Contact WordPress Directly

WordPress offers support, but it is directed to those who use the WordPress.com service, and not the self-hosted WordPress. You can reach the support team at http://en.support.wordpress.com/contact/.Before contacting WordPress support, make sure to perform some basic troubleshooting. Try looking in the WordPress documentation before reaching out to the support team.

## Search Engines

As mentioned previously, because WordPress is a blogging system, blogs are often a support form. When bloggers have trouble with WordPress and find a solution, there is a good chance they will blog about their experience.

Yahoo!, Google, Ask, and Bing are all great places to start your search for issues you have.

If you are doing searches about a particular feature, and not so much a problem, be sure to use the word WordPress in your search terms. For example, search "WordPress edit time stamp," and you get more results for exactly what you are looking for than if you just search for "edit time stamp."

Also, when you're searching for a solution to a specific error message you received, be sure to put the text of the error message in the search box, too. Adding this extra text can help narrow your search results to those that address exactly the error you are having an issue with.

Of course, searching with your favorite search engine will find not only pages and blog posts, but also forum results.

# Forums

WordPress hosts Official Support forums at http://wordpress.org/forums. These forums provide another great starting point. Usually, especially when you're starting out, you find other people have had the same or similar issues.

The big attraction to using the WordPress forums is that other users here share a common interest (WordPress) and are willing to help solve your problem. I have found other users to be friendly and generous.

The forums are free to read and search, but to participate in conversations, you need to create an account. It is quick and easy, and I highly recommended it.

After you register, you are sent an email with a password as a confirmation of your account.

Topics are logically laid out based on function from installation to troubleshooting to theming and plug-ins.

Before you start posting, here are some tips to get the most out of your forum experience:

▶ Search first. Spending a few minutes can save you and others time trying to figure out your issue. Often you can find an answer right away.

▶ Be descriptive. Describing your issue thoroughly can make the difference in explaining yourself three times and getting an answer right away. Be sure not to ask something like "Why doesn't my plug-in work?" Instead, explain which plug-in you are using and what you are trying to do. Also include version numbers, such as your WordPress version and the version of your plug-in. And use clear subject titles when creating a forum post.

▶ Show your issue. If the problem you are experiencing is visible on the Internet, include a URL or link to a screenshot. Diagnosing your issue is much easier if others can see it.

> ▶ Be patient and courteous. Remember the other users of the
> forums are there to help you at no cost. Often you might not get
> a response right away. You are on the other person's time if
> someone engages you to help with an issue.

# Paid Support

Regarding the nature of the issue you are having, an appropriate course of
action may be to contact someone at your hosting company. If you are
having trouble viewing your website or having other hosting matters not
related to WordPress directly, contacting paid support should be covered
under your monthly costs for web hosting.

Some companies and individuals prefer to rely on someone they can call
and ask for support, and that is certainly available. Depending on your
web host, it may provide services that assist in the installation or maintenance of your site for a fee, or perhaps it can recommend someone who
can.

Automattic (the company behind the hosting of WordPress.com) offers a
list of WordPress consultants from around the world at
http://codepoet.com/.

In addition, Automattic offers tiered levels of enterprise support for companies. The cost for this paid support service ranges from $15,000 to
$150,000. Automattic states that this support provides

> ▶ Access to several members of the WordPress development team
> to help you solve problems with your WordPress system
>
> ▶ Unlimited number of support incidents
>
> ▶ Software updates and upgrade notices
>
> ▶ Personal introductions to recommended third-party WordPress
> consultants and companies that offer custom development,
> design, and training

Automattic offers four tiers of support, each offering more features, better response times, and even site monitoring.

See Automattic's site for details at http://vip.wordpress.com/support/.

# Other Learning Resources

The following sources of support shouldn't be the places where you start searching for information, but they still provide excellent sources of information on what is happening in the world of WordPress.

## WordPress.tv

As stated on its site, WordPress.tv is "your visual resource for all things WordPress." This site has a lot of excellent videos posted that include how-tos, interviews, talks, and also videos featuring specific plug-ins.

If you navigate to http://wordpress.tv/category/how-to/, you can find lots of videos broken out into categories, which makes it easy to find videos on the specific topic you need.

## WordPress Lessons at the WordPress Codex

WordPress Codex offers a subset of some of the topics listed at the official WordPress documentation. These lessons range from installing WordPress to writing themes and plug-ins. You can find this site at http://codex.wordpress.org/WordPress_Lessons.

## NetTuts

If you are working on being a web developer, NetTuts is a valuable resource. On the NetTuts site, you can find articles regarding HTML, Ajax, JavaScript, PHP, and WordPress.

NetTuts offers tutorials for web developers and designers to help improve your work.

You can find the tutorials pertaining to WordPress at http://net.tutsplus.com/category/tutorials/wordpress/.

I have found these articles and screencasts to be very helpful in the past.

## Sams Teach Yourself WordPress in 10 Minutes 10 Minute Podcast

Chuck Tomasi and Kreg Steppe (the authors of this book) expand on some of the topics presented in this book and also keep you up to date on what's new in the world of WordPress, including releases, new features and interviews.

Visit http://www.chuckchat.com/wpin10 to keep current on WordPress.

## Summary

There is no shortage of WordPress help to keep you going when you need it. In this lesson, you learned many levels of support are available to you, ranging from forums, to blog posts, and even some paid support options. In addition, you were exposed to a lot of resources to continue your education in the world of WordPress.

# Index

## Q - R

## X - Y - Z

# FREE Online Edition

Your purchase of **Sams Teach Yourself WordPress in 10 Minutes** includes access to a free online edition for 45 days through the Safari Books Online subscription service. Nearly every Sams book is available online through Safari Books Online, along with more than 5,000 other technical books and videos from publishers such as Addison-Wesley Professional, Cisco Press, Exam Cram, IBM Press, O'Reilly, Prentice Hall, and Que.

**SAFARI BOOKS ONLINE** allows you to search for a specific answer, cut and paste code, download chapters, and stay current with emerging technologies.

## Activate your FREE Online Edition at www.informit.com/safarifree

> **STEP 1:** Enter the coupon code: FLHJZAA.

> **STEP 2:** New Safari users, complete the brief registration form. Safari subscribers, just log in.

difficulty registering on Safari or accessing the online
…e e-mail customer-service@safaribooksonline.com